WELL-BEING

Well-Being and Death addresses philosophical questions about death and the good life: what makes a life go well? Is death bad for the one who dies? How is this possible if we go out of existence when we die? Is it worse to die as an infant or as a young adult? Is it bad for animals and fetuses to die? Can the dead be harmed? Is there any way to make death less bad for us? Ben Bradley defends the following views: pleasure, rather than achievement or the satisfaction of desire, is what makes life go well; death is generally bad for its victim, in virtue of depriving the victim of more of a good life; death is bad for its victim at times after death, in particular at all those times at which the victim would have been living well; death is worse the earlier it occurs, and hence it is worse to die as an infant than as an adult; death is usually bad for animals and fetuses, in just the same way it is bad for adult humans; things that happen after someone has died cannot harm that person; the only sensible way to make death less bad is to live so long that no more good life is possible.

Well-Being and Death

BEN BRADLEY

CLARENDON PRESS · OXFORD

OXFORD

UNIVERSITY PRESS

Great Clarendon Street, Oxford OX2 6DP

Oxford University Press is a department of the University of Oxford.
It furthers the University's objective of excellence in research, scholarship,
and education by publishing worldwide in

Oxford New York

Auckland Cape Town Dar es Salaam Hong Kong Karachi
Kuala Lumpur Madrid Melbourne Mexico City Nairobi
New Delhi Shanghai Taipei Toronto

With offices in

Argentina Austria Brazil Chile Czech Republic France Greece
Guatemala Hungary Italy Japan Poland Portugal Singapore
South Korea Switzerland Thailand Turkey Ukraine Vietnam

Oxford is a registered trade mark of Oxford University Press
in the UK and in certain other countries

Published in the United States
by Oxford University Press Inc., New York

British Library Cataloguing in Publication Data
Data available

Library of Congress Cataloging in Publication Data
Data available

Typeset by SPI Publisher Services, Pondicherry, India
Printed in the United Kingdom by
Lightning Source UK Ltd., Milton Keynes

ISBN 978-0-19-955796-7 (Hbk.)
ISBN 978-0-19-959625-6 (Pbk.)

For Jackson and William

ACKNOWLEDGMENTS

I have been thinking and writing about death since roughly 2001, when I read a draft of Neil Feit's 'The Time of Death's Misfortune' and started coming up with my own ideas about death. Since then I have benefited from helpful feedback on my ideas about death and well-being from many colleagues, students, referees, editors, audience members, reading group participants, bloggers, friends, and enemies (you know who you are!). To those I have forgotten to single out by name here, I apologize.

I have presented ancestors of the material that appears here to audiences at Agnes Scott, Brown, Calgary, Cambridge, Idaho State, Kansas State, Macquarie, Missouri-Columbia, Nevada-Reno, North Carolina State, Oxford, Reading, Rochester, Stockholm, SUNY Buffalo, SUNY Fredonia, SUNY Geneseo, Syracuse, Virginia Tech, West Virginia, Western Washington, the 2001 Bellingham Summer Philosophy Conference, the 2004 APA Central Meeting, the 2004 and 2006 Creighton Clubs, the 2005 Inland Northwest Philosophy Conference, and the 2006 APA Pacific Meeting. I thank the audiences present on those occasions for their helpful comments. Thanks in particular to Jonas Åkerman, Mike Almeida, Gustaf Arrhenius, Tim Bayne, JC Beall, Chris Belshaw, José Benardete, John G. Bennett, David Braun, John Broome, Campbell Brown, Mark Brown, Mikel Burley, Tim Button, Krister Bykvist, Richard Chappell, Earl Conee, Roger Crisp, David DeGrazia, Jordan Dodd, Fred Feldman, Neil Feit, Greg Fitch, Bill FitzPatrick, André Gallois, Ernesto Garcia, Deke Gould, Sören Häggqvist, Peter Hanowell, Liz Harman, Jane Heal, Chris Heathwood, Mark Heller, David Hershenov, Brad Hooker, Dave Horacek, Frances Howard-Snyder, Larry James, Jens Johansson, David Kaspar, Simon Keller, Steve Kershnar, Shieva Kleinschmidt, Aaron Koller, Christian Lee, Barbara

Levenbook, Ken Lucey, Mark Lukas, Ishani Maitra, Ned Markosian, Kris McDaniel, Jeff McMahan, Peter Menzies, John Monteleone, Jonas Olson, Doug Portmore, Eric Rasmusen, Jonathan Schaffer, Kieran Setiya, Harry Silverstein, Peter Singer, Matt Skene, David Sobel, J. Howard Sobel, Roy Sorensen, Ernest Sosa, Joshua Spencer, Pablo Stafforini, Irem Kurtsal Steen, Jussi Suikkanen, Torbjörn Tännsjö, James Stacey Taylor, Matthew Tiffault, Christopher Williams, Fiona Woollard, and several anonymous referees for helpful comments and conversations.

Parts of this book have been adapted from 'A Paradox for Some Theories of Welfare' (*Philosophical Studies* 133 (2007): 45–53), 'When is Death Bad for the One Who Dies?' (*Noûs* 38 (2004): 1–28), 'Eternalism and Death's Badness' (forthcoming in Campbell, O'Rourke, and Silverstein (eds.), *Time and Identity* (Cambridge, MA: MIT Press)), 'The Worst Time to Die' (*Ethics* 118 (2008): 291–314), and 'How Bad Is Death?' (*Canadian Journal of Philosophy* 37 (2007): 111–27). Thanks to *Philosophical Studies*, *Noûs*, MIT Press, *Ethics*, and *Canadian Journal of Philosophy* for permission to use that material.

I have had the good fortune to be able to try out some of my arguments on the PEA Soup weblog (http://peasoup.typepad.com/peasoup/). Thanks to the PEA Soup community for the stimulating discussion there.

Thanks to the people at Oxford University Press, especially Peter Momtchiloff and Catherine Berry, for their assistance in bringing this book into existence.

This is the point in the acknowledgments where authors often thank the NEH or some other organization for giving them a fellowship to finish their book. Well, the NEH shot down my proposal for this book. So thanks for nothing, NEH! But thanks to Michael Zimmerman and Fred Feldman for their vain efforts on my behalf.

A few people deserve to be singled out for extra-special thanks for helping me get the manuscript into proper shape. Mikel Burley, Chris Heathwood, and Jens Johansson commented on multiple chapters of the book. Simon Keller, Roy Sorensen, and James Stacey Taylor graciously read and commented on the entire manuscript, as did the members of my death seminar at Syracuse in 2007: Andrew Corsa, Jeremy Dickinson, Anthony Fisher, Christina Hoffman, Kelly McCormick, John Monteleone, Jay Rourke, and Aaron Wolf. I thank all these people for their many helpful suggestions and probing criticisms. The book would have been much weaker, less interesting, and harder to understand without their help. Fred Feldman has provided invaluable guidance and assistance over the years. Much of this book is essentially a defense and refinement of some of Fred's views, though I should point out that Fred thinks some of my views are crazy. Finally, extra-extra-special thanks to my wife Cathy for her constant support.

CONTENTS

INTRODUCTION

The one aim of those who practise philosophy in the proper manner is to practise for dying and death.

Socrates[1]

Nobody holds Socrates' view about philosophy anymore. But death remains a rich source of philosophical questions. This book attempts to answer some of those questions. Is death bad for the person who dies? Under what circumstances is it bad? What makes it bad? How bad is it? Does the badness of death have a time—is it bad for us at some times but not others? Is it worse to die as a baby, a child, or an adult? Is it bad for animals to die? Is death less bad for someone who had a good life? Is there anything at all we can do to make our deaths less bad for us? If so, should we do it?

There is something weird about these questions. We would not ask these questions about other things we think are bad. Nobody could get away with writing a book about whether it is bad to stub your toe, what makes it bad, whether it is worse to stub your toe when you are a child or an adult, or whether we can make toe-stubbings less bad for us. Then how can I get away with writing this book? The answer is that, as we will see, the answers to these questions are somewhat less obvious concerning death than concerning toe-stubbings.

Death is an evil of deprivation. Dying keeps us from having more of a *good life*. So thinking about death leads us to think about what we think makes our lives go well for us. In Chapter 1 I attempt to develop some new arguments about the good life. These arguments tend to support hedonism, or the view that pleasure is what is good

---

[1] Plato, *Phaedo*, 64a.

for us and pain is what is bad for us. They support hedonism only indirectly, by posing problems for its main competitors, such as the view that what is good for a person is that she gets what she wants. Hedonism is often taken to have been thoroughly discredited. In fact, if a philosopher is asked to point out examples of truths that philosophers have conclusively established, the first would probably be that justified true belief is insufficient for knowledge;[2] the second might be that hedonism is false. Needless to say, I find this judgment to be premature, and hope that the arguments I provide will give pause to those who prefer other views about well-being. The arguments given here also undermine the possibility that events that take place *after* a person dies can affect her well-being.

According to the deprivation account of the evil of death, death is bad because it deprives us of a good life. Like most people, I accept that death is bad, and I accept the deprivation account of its badness. But there are versions of the deprivation account that differ in philosophically interesting ways. In Chapter 2 I argue for a *difference-making* account of deprivation, according to which the badness of a death is determined by a comparison between the life its victim actually lives and the life she would have lived had that death not occurred.

Death, I will assume, causes a person to go out of existence. So accounting for the evil of death requires us to engage with difficult metaphysical questions, such as: How can a nonexistent thing be the subject of a misfortune? Such questions do not arise when we talk about the evils of toe-stubbings; this is the most important difference between the two sorts of misfortune. Chapter 3 is largely concerned with questions about death and existence. In this chapter I argue against a view that I think has been rather dogmatically and uncritically accepted: that a dead person cannot have a well-being level, not even zero.

You might get lucky and never stub your toe as long as you live. But death is inevitable. Thus it is a universal object of fear. Socrates argued that philosophers in particular—but presumably everyone else too—should be unafraid of death. But this is because he thought

---

[2] Gettier 1963.

we survive our deaths, and that death is good for us.[3] Suppose that at death we permanently cease to exist. This thought can be terrifying. Is this terror rational? It is obviously rational to have an occasional worry about stubbing your toe. It hurts! But is it true, in general, that it is rational to fear (or otherwise have bad feelings about) something that is bad for us, even if it causes us no pain? I say a few things about this question in Chapter 2. But my main concern is the *badness* of death, and there is no necessary connection between the badness of an event and the rationality of fearing it. There is at least this connection though: if something is bad for you, then you have some (defeasible) reason to feel bad about it; and if something is not bad for you, then except in unusual circumstances, you have no reason to feel bad about it. Likewise, and more importantly, if something would be bad for you or someone else, then you have some (defeasible) reason to do something to prevent it.

Most would agree that death in old age is less bad for its victim than death as a young adult. But is it worse to die as a young adult than to die in infancy? This is another question that does not arise when thinking about toe-stubbings; nobody could really be puzzled over whether how bad it is to stub your toe depends on how old you are. In Chapter 4 I argue that death is typically worse the earlier it occurs, and so it is worse to die in infancy than as a young adult. Again, this seems to be a somewhat unpopular view (based on my informal quizzing of philosophers and their reactions to things I say), but the principles that philosophers have used in arguing for the opposite view are unsupportable.

Supposing death is a bad thing: what can we do about it? Is there anything we can do to make our deaths less bad for us? Some have thought that we can 'defeat' death by doing certain things in life, like completing our life's work. (This is another way in which death is unlike toe-stubbing. Nobody worries about whether it is possible to defeat toe-stubbings.) Unfortunately, those people are wrong. I

---

[3] Plato, *Phaedo*, 67d–e. In *Apology* 40c, Socrates takes seriously the possibility that there is no afterlife—that the dead are 'nothing' and have no sensation. He makes the astonishing claim that this would actually be *pleasant* for the nonexistent dead person, since it would be like a dreamless sleep, which we all recognize to be pleasant.

explain why in Chapter 5. It does turn out that there are things we can do to make our deaths less bad, but those are either things we have independent reason to do anyway—the fact that they tend to make our deaths less bad being irrelevant to whether we should do them—or things that would be obviously crazy to do.

So the main highlights of the book are as follows. I defend a straightforward *deprivation account* of the evil of death. This account has a controversial implication: *death is worse for its victim the earlier it occurs*. It also implies that how bad it is for a person to die does not depend, in any interesting way, on how well that person's life has gone. I also defend two views about well-being that very few people seem to hold: *hedonism* about the good life, and the view that dead people have a *zero well-being level*. Establishing the latter view enables me to defend another controversial view: that the badness of death has a temporal location. Death is bad for its victim at some time *after the person has died*.

There is an important question about death that I say absolutely nothing about in this book: What is death? I will take it for granted that we have enough of a grasp on the concept of death to get by. I will just make one assumption: death marks the end of a person's existence. This assumption might well be false. One way it would be false would be if people continue to exist as corpses after they die. This would make little difference to the arguments of this book. (If anything, the assumption that death marks the end of existence puts more pressure on my arguments in Chapter 3.) It hardly seems to make a difference to the badness of a person's death whether he is buried intact, thereby continuing to exist after death until natural processes and worms finish their work on him, or cremated, thereby going out of existence very quickly. On the other hand, perhaps people survive in some other form. Perhaps, as Socrates thought, people are composed of a body and a spirit, and the spirit survives the death of the body.[4] Or perhaps people survive their deaths without the benefit of a soul, by being resurrected or reincarnated; Locke argued for this possibility.[5] If some story like this were true, it would

[4] Plato, *Phaedo*, 64c.
[5] Locke, *An Essay concerning Human Understanding*, Bk. II, ch. xxvii.

put the arguments of this book in a different light. It would also make a big difference to the way we ought to feel about death, depending on what the afterlife is like. In fact, given some popular conceptions of the afterlife, the death of a person's body could be by far the best thing that ever happens to that person. But if this is true, then why is it so seriously wrong to kill people? In fact, why is it not frequently obligatory to kill people? If someone is a good person destined for heaven, it would seem best for that person if he were killed, painlessly, as soon as possible, since every day spent on earth is a day when that person is deprived of the infinite bliss of the afterlife.[6] So if we accept this view of the afterlife, any prohibition on murdering good people will not appeal to the fact that killing that person involves committing an act that is harmful to that person, all things considered. It would have to appeal solely to facts extrinsic to the person, such as harms to the person's family or to society. For the purposes of this book I assume that there is no afterlife—no souls, no resurrection, no reincarnation. But even those who believe in such things can endorse the general principles about value I defend here. They will just draw different conclusions from those principles. While I think the principles entail that death is usually very bad for people, those who believe in afterlives might think the opposite.

What we say about the value of life and the evil of death may be relevant to many other topics. First, our views about the good life help determine what we take to be prudent behavior. Those who think that it is intrinsically bad to have one's projects or desires frustrated might advise you not to cultivate desires that are unlikely to be fulfilled or embark on projects that are unlikely to be completed.[7] But if the arguments that follow are sound, this has at

---

[6] Of course, according to the worldview in question, no matter when the person died, he would get the same amount of afterlife bliss. This raises some tricky issues about infinite well-being that mirror problems about infinite utility faced by utilitarians. (See, for example, Kagan and Vallentyne 1997.) If the amount of well-being in the afterlife is the same no matter when death occurs, then killing neither harms nor benefits its victim—still a surprising implication. Thanks to James S. Taylor for discussion here.

[7] See Luper 2006. As Simon Keller pointed out to me, not all those who hold such views about well-being will give such advice.

best instrumental importance. Thomas Nagel thinks you are wasting your life if you spend all your time trying to communicate with asparagus plants—by which he means that your life is not going well for you, even if you're enjoying it.[8] I think Nagel is wrong about this. If you're like me, you will not enjoy talking to asparagus. (Not that I've tried, but is it hard to imagine?) But if you do enjoy it, you're not wasting your life unless you're bypassing some better opportunities in doing so.

One of the tasks of moral philosophy is to explain why killing is wrong, when it is wrong. The badness of death seems relevant to this question. This is not to say that the wrongness of a killing is always proportional to the badness of the death it causes, but there does seem to be some relationship here (as I've just briefly argued in discussing afterlives).[9]

One reason we may be interested in determining why killing is wrong, and hence in determining why death is bad, is to gain insight about topics of social concern, such as abortion and euthanasia. Suppose it is much worse to die in adulthood than in infancy. One might well think that it is even less bad to die as a fetus or an embryo. In that case, one might think abortion is not so bad. On the other hand, if it is worse to die as an infant than as an adult, it might be even worse to die as a fetus. If so, we might think abortion is seriously wrong. I think it may be extremely bad for a fetus to die—much worse than for an adult. This does not, however, show that aborting a fetus is wrong. I explain why in Chapter 4.

The value of death is naturally relevant to the question of whether euthanasia is morally permissible. The general principle I defend in this book entails that death may be good for people in some circumstances, e.g. when continued life promises more pain than pleasure. I think that in such cases, suicide is entirely rational, and assisting a person to commit suicide may be morally permissible or even obligatory. I also think it ought to be legal in at least some

---

[8] Nagel 1979, 5.

[9] For a very persuasive argument against the view that all killings of innocent people are equally wrong, see Lippert-Rasmussen 2007.

circumstances. All these points have, I think, been ably demonstrated by others, so I do not discuss them here.[10] I am of course not committed to the view that it is *always* permissible to kill someone in such circumstances. If the person does not wish to die, it may well be wrong to kill them out of paternalistic concern—certainly it should be illegal to do so.

What we say about the extent of death's badness has implications for what sorts of policies we should enact, and what sorts of things a society should spend money on. If it is worse to die as an infant than as an adult, as I argue in Chapter 4, then there is some reason to spend more money on curing illnesses that affect infants than on curing illnesses that affect only adults. That reason could well be outweighed by other factors, but it should be a factor in the equation.

What we say about why death is bad for people has implications for whether death is bad for non-human animals. David Velleman has argued that death is not bad for cows, since they have no ability to conceive of themselves as persisting through time.[11] My view entails that death is bad for cows as long as death deprives the cows of more of a good life. This does not necessarily mean that it is wrong to eat hamburgers, but it makes it harder to defend this practice. I discuss the badness of death for animals in Chapter 4.

What we say about posthumous harms has implications for policies and customs concerning the wishes of the dead. Since one upshot of my book is that the standard view of posthumous harm is untenable, we need to rethink policies and customs that require us to respect the wishes of the dead in order to avoid harming them. Of course, such policies and customs need not be justified by an appeal to posthumous harm. I discuss this at the end of Chapter 1.

So there are many good extrinsic reasons to think about questions about the evil of death. I just find the questions intrinsically interesting to think about. I have not written this book for the sake of answering any questions about social policy. But I hope that people who pick

---

[10] See, for example, Brock 1992.   [11] Velleman 1993, 354–7.

up this book out of interest in policy questions will end up being interested in the abstract philosophical questions too.

Finally, let me say a few words about my general philosophical strategy and methodology. The views I defend here are very simple. They are probably just about the simplest views one can hold that have any initial plausibility at all. I think simplicity is a very desirable feature of a theory. My aim is to take a handful of core insights and to formulate views that most accurately capture the ideas behind those insights, while completely eschewing any accretions or modifications that would give the appearance of *ad hoccery* in order to satisfy intuitions about particular cases. Most will find the resulting views far too crude. Pluralists will say there are many other things that are good for people besides pleasure. Others will say that the badness of death must be a far more complicated matter—that the badness of deprivation must be adjusted in various ways to account for intuitions about certain cases. I disagree. Sometimes we need to learn to live with the apparently counterintuitive implications of our philosophical theories when the alternative is to accept a convoluted monstrosity.

This insistence on simplicity is far from universally shared among philosophers, who sometimes insist that the truth of the matter about ethics must be complicated. To these philosophers, I can only say that complicated views always go wrong somewhere; where exactly they go wrong is often concealed by the complexity. The more complex the view, the more work it takes to draw out the unwelcome consequences—but they are always there. If you are not convinced of this as a general rule, perhaps you will be convinced by the particular arguments I present in what follows.

None of this is to say that I eschew appeal to intuitions. In fact, I appeal constantly to the reader's intuitions concerning, for example, whether some imagined death would be bad, and concerning the plausibility of the general principles I defend. Intuitions are sometimes thought to be of dubious value. Certainly we should not assume that things are the way they initially seem; our intuitions about cases are sometimes wrong. The 'James Dean Effect,' which I discuss in Chapter 5, is evidence of this. But some appeal to intuitions is unavoidable.[12] The trick is to rely on the right intuitions. On pain of contradiction, we cannot believe everything that seems true.[13] We have to make choices. The reader will be the judge of whether I have made the correct choices.

[12] For an excellent defense of the appeal to intuition in philosophy, and specifically in ethics, see Huemer 2005.

[13] For a helpful discussion of 'error theory' in ethics, with which I largely agree, see Kagan 2001.

I

WELL-BEING

The best thing for a man will be to live his life with as much joy as possible and as little grief.

Democritus[1]

1.1 The Concept of Well-Being

DEATH is typically one of the worst things that can happen to someone. It is bad for someone when it deprives her of a life that is good for her. But what makes someone's life go well for her?

Before we can answer this question, we need to clarify what we mean by 'well-being.' To that end, it would be helpful to have an *analysis* of the concept of well-being in terms of concepts that are more easily grasped. That is wishful thinking. But there are ways to get a grip on a concept even without an analysis. There are some features a good life typically seems to have. To see whether a life is good in the way we are interested in here, we can test it for those other features. That may give us some indication of whether it is good in the relevant sense.

Good lives are typically lives we *want* to live; when you want to know what sort of life is good for the person living it, it might be helpful for you to think about what sort of life you might like to have for yourself. But this is not a perfect test. For one thing, you might just be a bad judge of what is good for you. You might think

---

[1] Fragment 189; for discussion, see Kahn 1985, 27.

it would be good for you to get into the Guinness Book of World Records by spending the next several years grinding up and slowly eating a helicopter. But you would be wrong. For another thing, what you want for *yourself* depends on your own idiosyncratic likes and dislikes. You might have absolutely no desire to be a politician, but recognize that life as a politician could be a perfectly good life for someone else; or you might think it is essential to your own well-being that you be a doctor, without thinking that being a doctor is essential to everyone's well-being. So you might think a life is worth living without desiring it for yourself, and you might desire a life for yourself without thinking that others should desire it too.

It might be more helpful to think about what sort of life you would like for your newborn child, who has not yet formed any such idiosyncratic preferences.[2] But this is not a perfect test either. What we want for our children is not merely that they be well-off. Usually, we also want them to be good people, to do the right thing, and to make a positive impact on the world. It is not clear that these desires can be explained by appeal to our desire that our children be well-off. I would want my children to be good people even if this meant they would have to sacrifice their own well-being to some extent.

We might try to think about not just what we want for our children, but what we want for them *for their own sakes*. This might help avoid the problem just noted, but at a cost. The notion of a sake is too close to the very notion of well-being that we are trying to isolate. To want something for a person for her own sake is, it seems, to want it because of its effect on her well-being.[3] So whatever difficulty we might have in isolating the notion of well-being will remain in trying to isolate the notion of a sake. I find that it is often easier to tell what I want concerning my children than it is to tell whether I want those

---

[2] See Feldman 2004, 9–10, for more on the 'crib test.'

[3] It is actually not clear to me what we mean when we say we desire something for someone's sake. Perhaps desiring proposition P for the sake of person S involves having a desire that P that is *caused* by one's caring for S. (This seems to be suggested by Stephen Darwall (2002, 69).) Or maybe it involves having a sort of conditional desire: desiring that P on the *condition* that P enhances S's well-being. (See Bradley and McDaniel 2008 for more on conditional desires.) Or maybe it involves something else. I will not take a stand on this issue.

things for my children's sakes, or for someone else's sake, or for the world's sake.

Furthermore, my idiosyncratic likes and dislikes will extend to what I want for my children; I might recognize a certain life as being worth living, but not want it for my children simply because I have my own desires about how their lives turn out. And of course, if I wanted my children to grow up to eat helicopters, and thought this would result in good lives for them, I'd be just as wrong as if I wanted it for myself.

There might be no perfectly reliable way to isolate our judgments about well-being from other sorts of judgments. What we want for ourselves or others is an imperfect guide to our views about well-being. But it can at least help us to see what we are talking about when we talk about well-being. I will proceed on the hope that when we are assessing the value of someone's life, it is possible to determine whether we are making a judgment about what is good for the person living the life or about something else, and that thinking carefully about what we wish for ourselves and others can help us make this determination.

One might wonder about the possibility of a theory of well-being. It might be thought: *What counts as a good life for one person would not be a good life for someone else. For some people, having a lot of money is important. Others need to have lots of friends in order to live well, and do not care about money at all. Why think the same things must be good for all of us?* It is not easy to say what good lives have in common, but many worries about different things being good for different people can be put to rest by making a distinction between *intrinsic* and *extrinsic* value. Some things are good for us merely because they lead to other things that are good for us, or prevent things that are bad for us. These things are merely extrinsically good for us—more specifically, they are *instrumentally* good for us. They are good *as a means*. Money (or the having of it) is a good example of this sort of thing. If money did not enable me to buy things I want or need, it would be worthless to me. (Chapter 2 will be concerned with explaining the notion of instrumental value more carefully.) Other things would be good for us even if they did not lead to any other good things. These things are intrinsically good for us. What is intrinsically good for us is up for debate, but among the candidates frequently mentioned are pleasure, knowledge, achievement, and the satisfaction of preferences or desires. So, for example, if one person lives a good life by making lots of money, while another lives a good life by doing a job she enjoys, we might say that the reason they both live good lives is they are both getting what makes them pleased. Having money and having a good job are merely extrinsically good, while being pleased is intrinsically good (or so I will argue).

In this chapter I defend a hedonistic theory of well-being. Hedonism, roughly, is the view that pleasure is intrinsically good and pain is intrinsically bad, and (more controversially) that *nothing else* is intrinsically good or bad. As I've mentioned, hedonism is a very unpopular theory these days, and hedonists tend to spend a lot of time playing defense—showing how hedonism might be able to get around the various objections leveled against it, or attempting to minimize the importance of those objections.[4] I think the best defense is a good offense. So my defense of hedonism consists mostly of pointing out problems for hedonism's main competitors. By the end of this chapter, we will see that these arguments undermine the possibility of posthumous harm. In Chapter 3, we will see that these arguments also have implications for questions about the time of death's misfortune.

1.2 Theories of Well-Being

1.2.1 How to state a theory of well-being

Before we can go about stating a theory of well-being, we have to make a decision about how to talk. We have to decide what sorts of things, in the most general sense, we will take to be the bearers of intrinsic value. I will assume that the bearers of value are *states of affairs* as understood by Roderick Chisholm.[5] I identify states of

---

[4] For some recent defenses of hedonism, see Tännsjö 1998; Goldstein 1989; Feldman 2004; Crisp 2006; and Mendola 2006.

[5] See ch. iv of Chisholm 1976.

affairs with propositions; they are expressed by declarative sentences and 'that'-clauses (e.g., 'it is bad *that JFK was assassinated*'). Besides being bearers of intrinsic goodness, they are bearers of truth and falsity; when they obtain, they are true, and when they fail to obtain, they are false. They are fine-grained entities; *that JFK died* and *that JFK was assassinated by Oswald* are distinct states of affairs, since one has components that the other lacks, and the first could be true while the second is false (as conspiracy theorists claim). I choose to talk about theories of well-being in terms of states of affairs because it is standard procedure in the literature. I do not believe much turns on this decision. If you think the bearers of intrinsic value are events, or property instances, or some other sort of thing, feel free to make the appropriate translations.

When we state a theory of well-being, we are attempting to pinpoint those features of a life that are responsible for its value. More specifically, there are at least three things we must do in stating a theory of well-being. (1) First, we must say what sorts of states of affairs are intrinsically good or bad for us in the *most fundamental* way, or are *basically, non-derivatively*, good for us. Call these the *value atoms*.[6] The value atoms are what fundamentally and completely determine how well things go for us. (2) We must then say what determines *how* good or bad those atoms are. (3) Finally, we must say how to determine the values of non-atoms we might be particularly interested in. In particular, we must say how the values of complex things are determined by the values of the value atoms they contain. One of the non-atoms we may be interested in is *a person's life*.

The notion of a value atom requires some explanation. There are two conditions that states of affairs must meet in order to be value atoms. First, *their values are not determined by the values of their proper parts*. Some things are intrinsically good for us only because they have parts that are intrinsically good. Suppose I am happy right now and will be happy tomorrow at noon. Then there is an obtaining state of affairs consisting of me being happy now and me being

---

[6] For more on basic intrinsic value, see Harman 2000; Feldman 2000*a*; and Feldman 2004.

happy tomorrow at noon. That state of affairs is intrinsically good
for me. But it is not a value atom, because its value derives from the
values of its parts: the individual bits of happiness that compose it.
Perhaps those bits of happiness have basic intrinsic value for me, but
their conjunction does not. Second, the value atoms *incorporate all
the properties that are responsible for all the value there is*. If someone's
life is intrinsically valuable in virtue of instantiating some property,
that property will be incorporated into one of the fundamental value-
bearers. No relevant property will be left out. If two people's lives
differ in value, it must be because one has a property the other lacks;
that property must show up somewhere in our axiological theory, or
our theory is incomplete.[7] These conditions on value atoms will be
important to some of the arguments to come.

One may already be worried about my stage-setting. One might
say that the value of a person's life for her does not depend on the
values of its parts; lives have global features that determine their
values.[8] Compare two lives: the first begins with a terrible childhood
but gets better and better until it reaches a fabulous old age, while
the second begins wonderfully but gets slowly worse until it reaches
a terrible old age. Many people think the first would be better than
the second even if they contained the same amount of happiness.[9]
Call such people 'holists.' Holists need not find anything problematic
about the way I have set the stage. A holist can just say that the value
atoms may be very large, and that among the value atoms are entire
lives. But it is hard to believe that the value of a life could have *nothing*
to do with the values of its proper parts. If every moment of a life
is terrible, or even just mediocre, it could not be fantastically good
on the whole, no matter how well the parts fit together. The parts
make their own independent contributions to the value of the whole.
It is possible that the value of a whole life is determined by *both* the
values of its proper parts and its value taken as a whole, or its basic
intrinsic value.[10] On this view, value atoms can have other atoms as

---

[7] See Bykvist 1998, 44–5.

[8] On non-additivity, see Moore 1903; as this applies to whole lives, see Velleman
1993; MacIntyre 1981; and Brännmark 2001.

[9] C. I. Lewis 1946, 488; Velleman 1993.   [10] See Moore 1903, sect. 128.

parts. Questions about how to calculate the values of wholes based on their parts will be irrelevant in this chapter, so for now, I will assume that to get the value of any complex thing, we simply add the basic intrinsic values of all the atoms that compose it. This is for the sake of simplicity.[11]

An interesting question arises here: what is a person's life? Certain things seem clearly to be part of someone's life, such as her experiences of pleasure and pain. Others seem clearly not to be, such as facts about distant stars. How do we distinguish one from the other? We might say that a person's life consists of all those obtaining states of affairs that are directly about that person. But this would seem to include states that are only partly about me, and that intuitively do not seem to be part of my life. For example, my life would include the state of affairs *that Ben exists while the number of stars in the universe is even*. We might try to solve this problem by insisting that a person's life consists only of states of affairs that involve that person having some intrinsic property.[12] But this is far too restrictive; it entails that my getting married is not part of my life. I do not know of any good way to get around these problems, and I suspect that the attempt is pointless. There may be many notions of lives—biographical, biological, psychological, etc.—and I have no interest in picking one out as being particularly important. So I propose to bypass this discussion altogether by taking *worlds*, rather than *lives*, as the items of prudential evaluation.[13] We can say that a world is good or bad for a person without ever mentioning her life at all. The value of a world for someone is nothing mysterious; it is just how well things go for

[11] A related worry is: why assume there must be value atoms? What if value is infinitely divisible? The atomism assumption is for simplicity's sake. I take it that the views under discussion here could be reformulated without that assumption, though it may be hard in general to say how to do it.

[12] Hurka seems to identify a person's life with 'a sequence of states or events within [a person's] body' (Hurka 1998, 307).

[13] Another option is to take a person's life just to be whatever features of the world affect her well-being, as Broome does (Broome 2004, 94–5). This leads to some strange results, for example that two people could live the very same life. The difference here is merely terminological, but it seems better not to use the word 'life' in such an unconventional way if possible. In bypassing talk of lives, I also bypass the sorts of issues raised in Kagan 1994.

her at that world. The third component of a theory of welfare, then, tells us *the value of a world for a person* based on the basic intrinsic values for that person of the states of affairs obtaining at that world. And again, for simplicity, I assume that the value of a world for a person equals the sum of the basic intrinsic values, for that person, of the states of affairs obtaining at that world. For ease of exposition I will sometimes continue to refer to lives. But talk of the value of a life should be understood as talk about the subject-relative value of a world.

1.2.2 Hedonism

Hedonism is the view that states of affairs consisting of a person getting some pleasure—pleasure states—are the only positive value atoms, and pain states are the only negative value atoms. The idea that at least some pleasure is good and some pain is bad hardly needs justification; who would not want his child to be pleased at least sometimes? Who would wish her child to endure a life of pain? Just about everyone agrees that pleasure is *among* the intrinsic goods, even if few agree with the hedonist that *all* and *only* pleasures are intrinsically good.

One question confronting the hedonist is: what is pleasure? Is there really something in common between the various feelings and experiences that we call pleasant? Many have thought that pleasure is a sort of sensory feeling. However, it is difficult to isolate any such feeling common to pleasant experiences.[14] Consider how it feels to enjoy a game of tennis, and how it feels to enjoy a bowl of ice cream; it is hard to find any phenomenal feature in common between the two experiences. They just feel completely different.

Fred Feldman has argued that pleasure is a *propositional attitude*: an attitude that has a proposition as its object, like belief or desire.[15] When I enjoy playing tennis, what is happening is that I am pleased *that I am playing tennis, that I just hit a winning shot,* or *that I played an*

---

[14] See, for example, Sidgwick 1907, 127. But see Crisp 2006, 109–11, and ch. 4 of Mendola 2006 for recent challenges to the Sidgwickian view.

[15] Feldman 2004.

excellent point. This is of course not to say that there are no feelings occurring—I might feel sweaty, or tired, or exhilarated—but none of those feelings is the feeling of pleasure. Rather, I might be pleased *that I am having those feelings.* When one enjoys a bowl of ice cream, one takes pleasure in different feelings; the *feelings* are different, but it is the same *attitude* of pleasure. Analogous things might be said of pain.

There are other views about the nature of pleasure, such as views that analyze pleasure in terms of desire.[16] I do not wish to take a stand on the nature of pleasure, but it will be useful (and harmless, for our purposes) to suppose that the attitudinal account is true. So let us take hedonism to be the view that the value atoms are states consisting of a person taking pleasure or pain to some degree in some proposition.[17] All such pleasures are good, all such pains are bad, and there are no other good or bad value atoms. To distinguish this version of hedonism from other versions to be discussed, let us call this view *pure hedonism.*

Despite its initial appeal, few philosophers endorse pure hedonism. Perhaps the most notorious problem was raised by Robert Nozick in *Anarchy, State and Utopia*:

Suppose there were an experience machine that would give you any experience you desired. Superduper neuropsychologists could stimulate your brain so that you would think and feel you were writing a great novel, or making a friend, or reading an interesting book. All the time you would be floating in a tank, with electrodes attached to your brain. Should you plug into this machine for life, preprogramming your life experiences?[18]

Someone might get a lot of pleasure from being hooked to such a machine. If he were to spend the rest of his life hooked up to the machine, and his body were kept healthy, he might never experience much pain. Pure hedonism would count this as a great outcome for that person. But who, when looking down at her newborn child, would hope for him to live this way? Who would choose this life for herself? Movies like *The Matrix* enjoin us to think that this sort of life

---

[16] See, for example, Sidgwick 1907, 131.   [17] As in Feldman 2004.
[18] Nozick 1973, 42.

would be even worse than a dismal, desperate life in the real world. We might also imagine a person who believes that his family and friends like him, and takes pleasure in this, but is mistaken—in fact, they ridicule him behind his back, and only pretend to like him.[19] This is not the way we want things to go for ourselves or those we care about.

It is by no means obvious that these examples refute pure hedonism. Some would say that it makes sense to refuse to be hooked up to the experience machine even if being hooked up would be better for you. There are many reasons one might choose not to be hooked up. As I've noted, what we want for ourselves and others is not merely that we be well-off. We may desire to keep certain commitments that being on the machine would prevent us from keeping.[20] We may desire this not for our own sakes but for the sakes of others.

However, someone might well insist that even though he is aware of all the other reasons against choosing the experience machine life, he still finds it reasonable to reject the life merely on the grounds that it fails to be a good life *for him*, that he himself would be worse off on the machine than he would be living a normal life.[21] Perhaps this is what most people would think about the experience machine. At this point, I think the pure hedonist just has to admit that her view has some consequences that run contrary to common judgment. It is a revisionary view. This, by itself, does not provide sufficient reason to reject the view. We should not expect the true theory of well-being to be consistent with all of our intuitions about well-being, as there is little reason to think those intuitions are all true, or even consistent with each other. Any theory of well-being that has any initial plausibility or the slightest explanatory power will be revisionary in one way or another. Whether we should accept hedonism despite this apparently counter-intuitive implication depends upon what alternatives are available. So let us examine the alternatives.

[19] Nagel 1979, 4.
[20] Kawall 1999, 383–5. Also see Goldsworthy 1992, and Tännsjö 1998, 111–12. See ch. 3 of Bognar 2004 for criticism of these responses.
[21] See, for example, Griffin 1986, 9, and Sumner 1996, 97.

1.2.3 The alternatives

One might think that what is bad about life on the experience machine is the lack of connection between experience and reality. One's life is cut off from reality in a way that seems problematic; life becomes, in a way, *inauthentic*. If this is the problem with the experience machine, then we'd better build some experience-reality connection into our theory of well-being. There are several ways we might do this.

Feldman describes a way to be a hedonist but still deny that life on the experience machine is maximally good. We simply adjust the value of a pleasure depending on whether its propositional object is true or false.[22] Roughly speaking, a pleasure is more valuable when it is taken in a truth than when it is taken in a falsehood, so if Bobby and Cindy are both pleased that their friends like them, but Bobby's friends really like him while Cindy's do not, then things are going better for Bobby than for Cindy. Pleasure is still the sole intrinsic good; however, pleasure taken in a falsehood is less valuable or perhaps not valuable at all. Call this view *truth-adjusted hedonism*. Truth-adjusted hedonism preserves at least part of the hedonistic insight, but also entails that it is better for a person to be pleased when the things he is pleased about are facts rather than false propositions; thus, a life on the experience machine might be less good than a normal life, even if the experience machine subject takes greater pleasure in the propositions he believes to be true than does the subject of a normal life. One might prefer truth-adjusted hedonism to pure hedonism for this reason.

Some would say that what is bad about a life on the machine is it leaves many of our desires unsatisfied. On this view, what matters is getting what you want. We want to be actually doing the things we think we are doing; we do not want to be deceived about it; thus, when we are on the machine, we are not in fact getting what we want, even though it seems as if we are. *Desire satisfactionism* is the view that what makes a person's life go well is the satisfaction of her desires, and what makes it go badly is their frustration. For a desire

----

[22] Feldman 2004, 112.

to be satisfied is just for its propositional object to be true, and for it to be frustrated is for its object to be false.[23] The desirer need not have *feelings* of satisfaction or frustration, nor even know whether the desire is satisfied or not.[24]

Desire satisfactionists rarely endorse such a simple view. It is common to adjust the value of a desire satisfaction depending on, for example, whether the desire would remain if the desirer were to have complete factual knowledge about the world or were to undergo a course of cognitive psychotherapy.[25] Those who hold such views may be called *sophisticated desire satisfactionists*.

Closely related to desire satisfactionism is the view that *achievement* makes one's life go better.[26] Achievementists believe that one must put some effort into bringing about some outcome in order for that outcome to affect one's welfare, and that effort must actually play a role in bringing about the outcome. If I try very hard to get Obama elected president, and he is elected president but not because of anything I did, then I cannot be said to have *achieved* anything (even though I got what I wanted). Achievementism has some initial plausibility. Most of us want our children to have at least some modest amount of achievement; we do not want them to have everything in life handed to them, nor do we want their efforts to be in vain. There are few pure achievementists; most achievementists think achievement is only one of a number of things that are good for you. T. M. Scanlon, for instance, thinks

[23] This is a simplification. Kris McDaniel and I have argued that desires are directed at two propositions: an object and a condition (Bradley and McDaniel 2008). A desire is satisfied iff both its object and its condition are true; it is frustrated iff its object is false and its condition is true; it is cancelled iff its condition is false.

[24] Note that some have used the term 'fulfillment' to mean what I mean by 'satisfaction,' and use the term 'satisfaction' to mean something else entirely; see, e.g., Feinberg 1993, 177.

[25] See, for example, Brandt 1972. For a defense of the simpler version of desire satisfactionism, see Murphy 1999.

[26] Scanlon 1998, 118–23; Keller 2004. Rawls seems to have held something like this view; he says that a person's good consists of 'the successful execution of a rational plan of life' (Rawls 1971, 433).

achievements are intrinsically good for the achievers, but also thinks pleasure is intrinsically good.[27]

A life on the experience machine is likely to be very poor if achievementism is true, since the person in the machine is probably trying very hard to do various things, like play the piano or climb a mountain, but unbeknownst to her she is failing to do them. Achievementists who are pluralists, and who think pleasure is among the intrinsic goods, must say that life on the experience machine is excellent in at least one respect. But such a life turns out to be less good than it might have in light of the wasted 'efforts' undertaken while on the machine, and the lack of achievement the life contains. So perhaps achievementists gain an advantage over hedonists here. Whether the experience machine life turns out to be a good one depends on the importance of achievement relative to other intrinsic goods such as pleasure.

It should be noted that, just as few desire satisfactionists accept desire satisfactionism, achievementists are unlikely to accept the simplistic version of achievementism stated here. For example, Scanlon adjusts the value of an achievement depending on features of the thing achieved, so that it is better if the thing achieved is more 'comprehensive,' or more 'rational.'[28] We might also wish to adjust the value of an achievement for the extent to which the efforts of the achiever make a difference, so that the more important the efforts are, the more valuable the achievement. Let us call this family of views *sophisticated achievementisms*.[29]

Finally, some might think that what is disturbing about life on the machine is that many of one's beliefs turn out to be false. One believes that one is climbing a mountain, making friends, and playing the piano, but one is in fact doing none of those things. On this view, having true beliefs is intrinsically better than having false beliefs.[30]

---

[27] Scanlon 1998, 123.   [28] Scanlon 1998, 121–2.

[29] For a helpful taxonomy of achievementisms, see Portmore 2007*b*.

[30] See Moore 1903, ch. vi; Ross 1988, 138–40; Hurka 2001; 12–13; Keller (manuscript). Stephen Hetherington seems to hold a view along these lines as well (Hetherington 2001).

Call this *true beliefism*. Like achievementists, true beliefists typically think that true belief is just one good thing among many. True beliefism is, at best, part of the correct theory of welfare. But if a theory entails true beliefism, it has the resources to explain why we think life on the experience machine is lacking something important. Of course, it is not clear that any such theory will entail that a life on the experience machine is not a good life; it depends on what the other components of well-being are, and on the importance of true belief relative to those other components.

We now have five more-or-less explicitly formulated views on the table: pure hedonism, truth-adjusted hedonism, desire satisfaction-ism, achievementism, and true beliefism. Here is a recap, with some added detail about value atoms.[31]

Hedonism: the good (bad) value atoms are pleasure (pain) states. Pleasure (pain) states consist of a person taking pleasure (pain) to degree D at some time in some proposition; the value of such an atom equals D $(-D)$.[32]

Truth-adjusted Hedonism: there are two kinds of good value atoms: true pleasures and false pleasures. True pleasures consist of a person taking pleasure to degree D at some time t in some proposition P, and P. False pleasures consist of a person taking pleasure to degree D at time t in P, and not-P. There is one kind of bad value atom: a pain state.

Desire Satisfactionism: The good (bad) value atoms are desire sat-isfactions (frustrations). A desire satisfaction (frustration) is a state

---

[31] Note that most of these views are formulated in a way that presupposes a level of precision in assignments of intrinsic values to states of affairs. Some will find this silly; it may seem absurd, for example, to suppose that the intrinsic value of one state of affairs is precisely 2.37 times greater than the intrinsic value of another. Whether this is realistic or not, it is helpful in formulating a theory of well-being. For a defense of the use of numbers in axiology, see Hurka 1993, 86–8.

[32] On this way of understanding the view, we need to think of times as being larger than point-sized. Otherwise we run into pretty obvious problems when trying to add up the values of the basically intrinsically good states. This assumption will need to be made for every theory under discussion here.

consisting of a person desiring to degree D at time t that P, and P (not-P). Its value is D (−D).[33]

Achievementism: Among the good (bad) value atoms are achievements (failures). Achievements consist of (i) a person putting effort to degree D at some time t into seeing to it that P; (ii) P; and (iii) the person's effort helping bring it about that P. Failures consist of a person putting effort to degree D at time t into seeing to it that P, and not-P.[34] The value of an achievement (failure) equals D (−D).

True Beliefism: Among the good (bad) value atoms are true (false) beliefs. True (false) beliefs consist of a person believing at some time t that P, and P (not-P).

There are many other theories out there as well.[35] As previously noted, there are sophisticated versions of desire satisfactionism and achievementism. There is also another view I've alluded to and should be treated separately: pluralism, or the 'objective list' theory.[36] According to pluralism, there are several sorts of value atom, perhaps including pleasures and pains, achievements and failures, and true and false beliefs. I take it that while each monistic view has its defenders, pluralism is the most popular view about well-being. It is not hard to see why: it inherits the initial plausibility of each of the monistic views it subsumes, and does not force us to choose sides.

[33] Krister Bykvist pointed out to me that a desire satisfactionist might instead hold that there are distinct mental states of desire and aversion, and that the bad value atoms consist of someone having an aversion to P when P is the case (rather than desiring P when P is not the case). I do not think this would make a difference to what happens in this chapter.

[34] See Keller 2004, 36.

[35] One notable theory I have not explicitly discussed is perfectionism; see Hurka 1993 for a detailed exposition and defense. Since achievement and knowledge are part of Hurka's notion of perfection, Hurka's perfectionism encounters all the problems I raise for these views here. Hurka explicitly denies that perfectionism is a theory of well-being.

[36] Parfit 1984, 499–501; Hurka 2001, 12; Ross 1930, 134–41; Scanlon 1998, 124–5. It is not clear that Parfit and Hurka would actually endorse OLT. Parfit seems more inclined towards something like Feldman's view, while Hurka seeks to unify at least some of the components of the list through his perfectionist theory (Hurka 1993).

The advantages of pluralism should not be oversold, for it is vulnerable to many of the problems of the subsumed monistic views. For example, if one rejects pure hedonism on the grounds that false or immoral pleasures are worthless, the move to pluralism offers no help unless (implausibly) pleasure is not on the list. If one is worried about achievementism or true beliefism in light of examples of people who know or achieve lots of things but never get any enjoyment out of it, the move to pluralism again offers no help. At best, pluralism mitigates these problems somewhat. For example, it presumably ranks the life with lots of knowledge, but no pleasure, lower than a life with the same amount of knowledge but lots of pleasure, and ranks the experience machine life lower than a life with the same amount of pleasure and pain, but more knowledge.

And pluralism has its own unique problems. For one thing, pluralism seems objectionably arbitrary. Whatever the composition of the list, we can always ask: why should these things be on the list? What do they have in common? What is the rational principle that yields the result that these things, and no others, are the things that are good?[37]

For another thing, pluralists must tell us, for example, how to compare the effect on well-being of a certain amount of pleasure with the effect of a certain amount of knowledge. This problem has so far proved intractable. W. D. Ross attempted to solve this problem, and was led to an absurd lexical ordering view.[38] As far as I can tell, little or no progress has been made on the weighing problem in the ensuing 78 years. Rather, it is now common for pluralists to assert that no such weighing is possible.[39]

To the extent that the pluralist refuses to tackle these questions she abandons the philosophical project of understanding well-being; she admits defeat. A theory that tells us that A, B, and C are intrinsically good, but does not tell us why those things are on the list or how to weigh them, does not give us what we initially wanted out of a theory of well-being. We wanted enlightenment, but we are provided

[37] See Hurka 2001, 244 for a similar complaint about list-based theories of virtue.

[38] Ross 1930, 149–54.

[39] See, for example, many of the entries in Chang 1997.

instead with a list, and are told not to look any deeper. This is not theorizing, but a refusal to theorize.

In what follows I will not treat pluralism as a distinct theory, since in the absence of a weighing principle, we do not have a theory with any testable implications at all. However, some of the arguments in this chapter will apply, with minor modifications, to any version of pluralism that includes desire satisfaction, achievement, or true belief among the goods.

We may divide theories of welfare into two groups. On the one hand, we have several theories—truth-adjusted hedonism, desire satisfaction, achievementism, and true beliefism—that attempt to provide ways to explain the fact that the experience machine life is less good than an experientially similar non-machine life, by building in some sort of experience-reality connection.[40] These theories share an important feature. In each case, the value atoms have two parts. One part consists of someone having some propositional attitude (taking pleasure in, desiring, pursuing, or believing something). The other consists of the propositional object of that attitude being true (for intrinsic goods) or false (for intrinsic bads). Call these theories 'correspondence theories.' On the other hand, we have pure hedonism, which takes atomic states of affairs to be the value atoms.

Correspondence theories are of particular interest when discussing death. If a correspondence theory is true, it may be possible for events taking place after a person dies to affect, retroactively, how well that person's life went for him. For example, according to desire satisfactionism, if a person desires to be cremated after she dies, the value of her life will depend in part on whether she is cremated. This would not be the case according to pure hedonism, since whether she is cremated or not could not possibly affect her experiences of pleasure or pain. The compatibility of desire satisfactionism with posthumous harm is sometimes viewed as an advantage of desire satisfactionism over hedonism.[41] If failing to respect the wishes of the

---

[40] For arguments along these lines for correspondence theories see Bigelow, Campbell, and Pargetter 1990.

[41] Feinberg 1993; Pitcher 1993; and Luper 2004 are just a few prominent examples of the attempt to account for posthumous harm by appeal to desire frustration.

dead can affect their welfare, then there is an important reason to respect their wishes. If not, we must find another justification, or else conclude that no such reason exists.

Correspondence theories face some important problems. I will discuss two problems that have not received much attention from well-being theorists. I find these problems to be so serious that correspondence theories should be rejected. This will provide indirect support for pure hedonism. Some will find the problems I raise here less compelling than the problems pure hedonism faces with experience machines, and others will prefer to look for a non-correspondence theory other than pure hedonism. Nevertheless, the problems must be taken seriously.

1.3 Well-Being and Time

A person's whole life, or a world, can go well or badly for her. But parts of lives, or *times*, can go well or badly for a person too. Things go well for a person at some times and badly at others. When we say that someone is having a bad day, or the time of her life, we are not speaking metaphorically; what we say is, at least sometimes, literally true. Pure hedonism can account for temporal facts about welfare in a straightforward way: the good times in a person's life are the times when she is pleased; the bad times are the painful times. The story is simple because the time a pleasure is good for me is just the time of the pleasure, and pleasures are in principle easily locatable in time. The value of a time for a person is determined by the values of the pleasures and pains experienced by that person at that time. So pure hedonism is compatible with the following principle:

Internalism. The intrinsic value of a time for a person is determined entirely by the value atoms obtaining at that time.

For a contrary view of the matter, see Overvold 1980, 108, and Taylor 2005. For arguments that desire satisfactionism cannot account for posthumous harm, see Portmore 2007a.

As John Broome puts it, 'how well off a person is at a time depends only on how things are for her at that time.'[42] Why accept internalism? Internalism follows from a more general supervenience principle closely related to one endorsed by G. E. Moore:[43]

SUP. The intrinsic value of something depends solely on its intrinsic properties.

If SUP is true, the intrinsic value of a time is determined by its intrinsic nature—not by anything happening at any other time.

Nowadays, it is common to reject SUP.[44] But SUP is a requirement of any acceptable theory of well-being. This is because, as noted above, the value atoms should be *instantiations of the fundamental good- or bad-making properties*—the properties that are fundamentally and completely responsible for how well a world (or a life, or ...) goes. Suppose SUP were false. Then there could be two properties, F and G, such that the only intrinsically good states of affairs are those involving the instantiation of F alone, but whose values are determined by whether there are any instantiations of G. But if that were true, F would fail to be a *fundamental* good- or bad-making property, for instantiations of F would fail to completely determine what value there is. The fundamental good- or bad-making property would involve both F and G, contrary to our assumption. Once we are committed to the project of finding the fundamental good- and bad-making properties—the fundamental project of axiology, and of the theory of well-being—we are immediately committed to SUP, and therefore to internalism.

Another reason to accept internalism is that it helps us to solve a puzzle raised by Epicurus. For this solution, the reader will have to wait until Section 3.3.

Before proceeding, let me preempt some worries about internalism. First, we need not assume that every intrinsically good state of affairs affects how things go for a person at a particular time; for example, if facts about the upward or downward trajectory of a life affect the

---

[42] Broome 2004, 101.   [43] Moore 1922, 260.
[44] See Korsgaard 1983; Kagan 1998; Hurka 1998; Rabinowicz and Rønnow-Rasmussen 1999; and Olson 2004a.

value of the life, they do not seem to make any particular time in the life go better. The holist will just deny that the value of a life is determined entirely by the values of its moments taken individually. This is compatible with internalism as I have formulated it. So no questions have been begged against holistic views.

Second, one might notice that there seem to be many cases when we think that how things went yesterday help determine how well things are going for me now, and one might think this poses a problem for internalism. Suppose that yesterday I drank a poison that always causes intense stomach pain 24 hours after ingestion. My drinking the poison yesterday helped determine how badly things go for me today. But this is no counterexample to internalism. There is a difference between *constitutive* and *causal* determination. When I say that the intrinsic value of a time is determined by the value atoms obtaining at that time, I mean that once the value atoms obtaining at a time have been fixed, the value of that time has also been fixed. To determine how badly things go for me today, it is sufficient to know how much pain I'm in today (along with any other intrinsically bad things that happen to me today). Drinking the poison yesterday *caused* today's pain, but does not itself *enter into the determination of* the value of today for me. Given that I'm in pain today, things are no better or worse for me today because the pain was caused by poison.

It may also be thought, contrary to internalism, that how things turn out later could help determine how well things are going now.[45] Suppose Kate is a pianist, and will be giving a big performance at the end of September. She practices hard, making many sacrifices, during September; as a result, she gives a spectacular performance, and this is a very good thing for her. We might well say that her practicing was a good thing for her, or that things were going well for her during the month of September. But of course this might mean different things. It might mean that things were going *intrinsically* well for her—that she was well-off during the practicing time—or it might mean that things were going *instrumentally* well for her—that things were happening that would make things go intrinsically better for her later. Surely the second is the more natural thing to say.

---

[45] Thanks to Simon Keller for discussion of this point.

During the concert we might well say that *all her hard work is paying off now*; we might say that it is good that she worked so hard before, or more stiltedly, that her previous hard work had *instrumental* value as a result of what is now happening. It is much stranger to say that her current performance is *paying off her past self*, in the sense that it is retroactively making her better off in the past. If Kate's performance made it the case that she was well-off while she was practicing over the previous month, it would be hard to see her practicing as involving a sacrifice of current well-being for future well-being, since her 'sacrifice' would have been beneficial to her at the very time she was practicing.[46] So there is no good reason to reject internalism on the basis of such examples.

Correspondence theorists have problems accounting for the truth of internalism. Consider desire satisfactionism. Suppose we ask: when is a desire satisfaction good for me? Is it at the time of the desire or at the time I get the thing I desired? This question turns out to be very difficult to answer.[47] Remember that desire satisfactionism, and all correspondence theories, take the value atoms to be *compound states*: states of affairs that are conjunctions of someone having a propositional attitude (desire, belief, pleasure ...) directed at a proposition P, and P being true.[48] Suppose the person has the attitude at time t_1 and the object obtains at later time t_2. When does their conjunction obtain? It does not obtain at t_1; only part of it does. The same goes for t_2. It is perhaps best to say that the conjunction obtains at the fusion of t_1 and t_2—that is, at the smallest, possibly discontinuous, time that has t_1 and t_2 as parts. So if internalism is

---

[46] David Velleman and Doug Portmore argue that future successes may redeem past sacrifices (Velleman 1993; Portmore 2007*b*). However, even Velleman and Portmore do not seem to think that future successes can make past sacrifices have less of a negative impact on momentary well-being. Rather, they think future successes can make past sacrifices have less of a negative impact on *lifetime* well-being. So their views seem to be compatible with internalism. Jeff McMahan, on the other hand, explicitly claims that future events may affect past momentary well-being (McMahan 2002, 180).

[47] See Baber (forthcoming) for an extensive discussion of this problem.

[48] Note that this same problem threatens any view that takes compound states as basic, not just correspondence views. But the most popular views that take compound states as basic are correspondence views.

true, then if the conjunction affects S's well-being at any time, it must be at the fusion of t₁ and t₂—not at t₁ itself, nor at t₂ itself. If this is so, then it seems difficult for things to be going well or badly for a person at any moment—only at fusions of moments (and disconnected fusions of moments, at that).

There are two options for a correspondence theorist who wishes to endorse internalism and also wants to account for momentary well-being.

Concurrence. The first option for the correspondence theorist is to insist that the attitude and its object must be *concurrent* in order for the satisfaction, achievement, or true belief to be good. You have to get what you want (or are aiming for, or believe, or take pleasure in) when you want it (or aim for, believe, or take pleasure in it). This idea has some independent plausibility, for as Chris Heathwood points out, 'If I desire fame today but get it tomorrow, when I no longer want it, my desire for fame was not satisfied.'[49]

The concurrence requirement makes desire satisfactionism incompatible with posthumous harm. We could not say, for example, that posthumous desire satisfactions make a person's life go better, since the desire does not overlap with the obtaining of its object. The correspondence theorist might be willing to accept that posthumous harm is impossible, and I cannot take issue with the correspondence theorist on that score.

But other problems will remain. For one thing, the concurrence view does not go well with some correspondence theories. Take achievementism, for instance. It seems that the efforts put in to achieve something often do not overlap in time with the obtaining of the object of the efforts; nor does anyone particularly care whether they do. But if the concurrence thesis were true, we should care quite a lot, since only in cases of overlap would an achievement affect momentary well-being. A weightlifter might get lots of well-being from his achievements, since his efforts and his achievement overlap while he is straining to keep the weight aloft; but a golfer would get

---

[49] Heathwood 2005, 490.

no well-being from hitting a hole in one, since her efforts happen entirely before the payoff. This is a bizarre result. Nobody thinks weightlifting contributes more to well-being than golf does—not on *those* grounds, anyway.

In general, no matter which sort of correspondence view we consider, if it is combined with a concurrence thesis, there will be far less momentary well-being than we might have thought. For if we adopt a concurrence version of desire satisfactionism, desires about the past and future cannot affect our well-being. But why should this be? Surely a great many of our desires are future-directed. None of these desires would affect our well-being given the concurrence thesis.

The desire satisfactionist might say that all desire satisfactions and frustrations affect one's lifetime well-being, but only in cases of concurrence do they affect *momentary* well-being. But in many cases it seems counterintuitive to think that concurrence makes a difference at all, either to lifetime well-being or to momentary well-being. When one *does not know* when one's desire has been satisfied or frustrated, it is natural to say that it does not matter whether the desire and its object overlap in time. Here is a pair of cases described by Joel Feinberg. In the first case, a woman has a desire; before she dies, her desire is frustrated, but she never finds out about its frustration. The second case is exactly like the first except that the desire is frustrated shortly after she dies.[50] There seems little reason to think that one of these lives is better than the other, or that one had better moments.

There is a way to finesse the problems I have raised. The trick is to take the time the propositional object obtains as the time(s) at which the propositional object is *true*.[51] To see how this works, consider desire satisfactionism. Suppose Cathy currently desires to see a concert next week. The object of her desire is the proposition: that

---

[50] Feinberg 1993, 181–2. Also see Fischer 2006, 360 for a similar example.

[51] Thanks to Doug Portmore for this suggestion. The strategy described here is essentially the one employed by George Pitcher, and endorsed by Steven Luper, in accounting for posthumous harm; see Pitcher 1993, 166–8, and Luper 2004.

Cathy sees a concert next week. Suppose Cathy will in fact see a concert next week. Then Cathy's desire is satisfied, and, in a sense, the desire and its object obtain at the same time: now. She desires, *now*, to see the concert next week, and it's true, *now*, that she *will*. Suppose it is not true, now, that Cathy will see a concert next week. Then her desire is frustrated, and the desire is simultaneous with the non-obtaining of its object. This provides a way to put desires about the future and past on a par with desires about the present. We might say the same thing about other correspondence theories.

But this strategy disguises what is really going on when a desire is satisfied. When Cathy now desires that she see a concert next week, it may be true now that she will see a concert next week; but it is true in virtue of what happens *next week*, not in virtue of anything happening right now. Given Cathy's desires, and given the truth of desire satisfactionism, the features of the world that make the world good for Cathy include her *current* mental state and concert-related events occurring *next week*. Thus, we do not say that Cathy's desire *has already been satisfied* in virtue of the future being the way it is. We say it has not yet been satisfied, but will be satisfied (or frustrated) next week. So we must take the time P obtains to be the time when P's *truthmaker* happens, rather than the time(s) at which P is true. Since desires about the past and future have past and future truthmakers, they cannot be concurrent with their objects in the sense that matters.[52]

Some cases of desire satisfactions, such as the desire that π be irrational, do not involve a datable truthmaking event. Furthermore, in most cases of desire frustration, there will not be a datable event to serve as the falsifier of the propositional object of the desire. If I desire to climb Mount Everest before I die, but never do, there will probably not be an event to identify as the event in virtue of which my desire is frustrated (unless, for example, I am hit by a falling rock on my way up). This merely introduces further complications for the desire satisfactionist in accounting for momentary well-being. Similarly, it seems, for all correspondence theories.

[52] Thanks to David Braun and Chris Heathwood for discussion of this issue.

There is another worry about concurrentism. Suppose that, as Einstein suggested, there is no such thing as 'absolute simultaneity'— that is, suppose that concerning events occurring at different spatial locations, there is no absolute fact of the matter about whether they occur at the same time.[53] If this were so, a person's well-being level at a time would be relative to a reference frame. For example, if I have a desire that some event take place on the sun, and it does take place, there would be no absolute fact of the matter about whether this affected my well-being or not, because there would be no fact of the matter about whether my desire and the solar event were simultaneous. This is a very odd result. I am not qualified to pass judgment on controversial issues in relativity theory. But I would not want to be in the position of endorsing a theory of well-being whose plausibility depends on deep scientific truths that are hotly contested. For even if there is actually such a thing as absolute simultaneity, surely there is some possible world where there is not. A theory of well-being should be necessarily true if true at all. So it does not matter which side is actually right about absolute simultaneity; the mere fact that things might have been the way apparently suggested by Einstein undermines concurrentism. The concurrence view should be rejected.[54]

Reformulating the theories. The other move for the correspondence theorist is to deny that the value atoms are conjunctions. There are two options here. Either we take the value atoms to consist only of an attitude, or we take them to consist only of the object of the attitude. Call the former view *attitudinalism*, and the latter view *objectualism*. Which way is more plausible to go here depends on the relevant attitude. Some attitudes are said to have a 'mind–world' direction of

---

[53] On simultaneity see Janis 2006.

[54] Torbjörn Tännsjö suggested to me that if we restrict the desires that affect one's well-being to *self-regarding* desires, we may avoid some of the problems I have raised for the concurrence view, such as the Einstein problem. But it is not clear to me that this would help very much, unless self-regarding desires are to be understood as desires concerning only events happening entirely within one's own body. And I do not believe desire satisfactionists would be happy to say this.

fit, while others have a 'world–mind' direction of fit.[55] Beliefs have a mind–world direction of fit; beliefs are successful when they conform to the way the world is. When we ask when a person had a true belief, the natural answer is that it is at the time of the belief; that's when the person got her beliefs in conformity with the world. Desires have a world–mind direction of fit; desires are successful when the world conforms to them. When we ask when someone had a desire satisfied, the natural answer is that it is at the time the object of the desire obtained, because that's the time when the world conformed itself to her desire. Thus it seems best for the desire satisfactionist to agree with David Velleman when he says: 'Nor do we say, of a person raised in adversity, that his youth was not so bad, after all, simply because his youthful hopes were eventually fulfilled later in life. We might say that such a person's adulthood compensated for an unfortunate youth, but we would not say that it made his youth any better.'[56]

Pleasure seems more like belief with respect to direction of fit, since we should (allegedly) adjust our pleasures to the truth, while achievement seems more like desire, since we achieve things by manipulating the world to conform to our attitudes. The suggestion, then, is that the desire satisfactionist and the achievementist should be objectualists, and say that the value atoms are not wholes consisting of a desire and its object being satisfied, but merely obtainings of the *objects* of desires.[57] Conversely, true beliefists and truth-adjusted hedonists should be attitudinalists. So, for example, if desire satisfactionism is true, and I desire to eat French fries tomorrow, my eating French

---

[55] This distinction derives from a discussion on p. 56 of Anscombe 1957. As Copp and Sobel note, talk of direction of fit may be no more than 'a metaphor that can give an intuitive sense of the difference between belief and desire' (Copp and Sobel 2001, 52).

[56] Velleman 1993, 340. Also see Portmore 2007a.

[57] See Rabinowicz and Österberg 1996 for an explicit formulation of this view, and Baber forthcoming, 22–3 for a related view. It is common for philosophers to implicitly assume that this is how the view ought to be formulated; for two examples, see Glannon 2001, 131, and Velleman 1993, 401 n. 45. Baber claims that 'an individual benefits from posthumously satisfied desires when, after his death, the states he desires come to be' (forthcoming, 23), but it is not clear whether she thinks the individual's well-being level rises at that time.

fries tomorrow is intrinsically good for me; the relevant value atom is just the state of affairs *that Ben eats French fries*. If true beliefism is true, and I believe the sun will rise tomorrow, *my belief itself* is intrinsically good for me if the sun rises tomorrow, and is intrinsically bad for me if it does not.

The resulting views are compatible with internalism. However, they should be rejected. Let us begin with objectualism. Objectualism has some very odd consequences concerning momentary well-being. For example, suppose that Abraham Lincoln desired that an African-American be elected President of the United States one day, and suppose Barack Obama wins the 2008 election. If objectualism is true, then Obama's winning the election in 2008 is a positive value atom for Lincoln. And if internalism is true, it follows that Lincoln has a positive well-being level in 2008. But this is absurd. Even worse, suppose John McCain is conducting a genealogical investigation, and desires that his ancestors did not own slaves. Objectualism entails that McCain was well-off or badly-off (depending on facts about his ancestors) *hundreds of years before he even came into existence*. This is sufficient reason to reject objectualism.

Next let us turn to attitudinalism. Unlike objectualism, attitudinalism can account for the possibility of posthumous harm or benefit without entailing that a person's well-being level rises and falls after she dies. The time of the harm or benefit is while the individual is alive and having the relevant attitude.

However, attitudinalism entails that the value of a state of affairs may depend on the obtaining of a wholly distinct state of affairs. For example, according to the attitudinalist version of true beliefism, the value of my current belief that the sun will rise tomorrow depends on whether the sun rises tomorrow. Thus attitudinalism is incompatible with SUP, which I have argued is a non-negotiable axiological principle. One way to see the problem is this: If attitudinalism were true, it would be possible for two lives to contain *exactly the same value atoms*, yet have different values. That should not happen if we've determined the value atoms correctly and completely. To further clarify: the problem with attitudinalism is that it shifts the good-making properties out of the value atoms themselves and into other states that determine the values of the atoms. Whatever we choose to

call the 'value atoms,' the attitude itself is not the fundamental good-
or bad-making property. The fundamental good-making property
includes both the attitude and its object. So what is at issue is no
longer when the value atom obtains, but when the fundamental good-
making property is instantiated. It is not at the time of the attitude
(except in cases of concurrence). Keeping the object of the attitude
out of the value atom does not change the answer to the question
at hand—it merely disguises the answer. Attitudinalism must be
rejected. This point applies to objectualism as well, since according
to objectualism, whether P's obtaining is intrinsically good for S
depends on whether S has the relevant attitude towards P.

We've looked at two ways for correspondence theorists to attempt
to account for momentary well-being while accepting internalism:
adopt a concurrence requirement, or modify the theory in such
a way that conjunctions are not the value atoms. Both ways are
problematic. Thus I find no plausible way for the correspondence
theorist to account for the times of benefits and harms. And moving
to 'sophisticated' correspondence theories offers no help, because
whether a goal is comprehensive, or the object of desire is rational,
makes no difference to any of the arguments just presented.

This criticism might seem unfair, given the way I set the stage in
Section 1.2.1. A theory of well-being, I said, answers three questions:
(1) What are the value atoms? (2) How good or bad are the value
atoms? (3) What determines the value of a whole life—or the value for
a person of a whole world? I have not yet shown that correspondence
theories answer any of these questions wrongly. What I'm suggesting
is that a complete theory of well-being must also answer a fourth
question: (4) What determines the value of a moment or period
of life? I have argued that correspondence theories cannot give a
plausible answer to this question.

The correspondence theorist might engage in a strategic retreat
here. He may admit that he cannot answer (4), but maintain
that he can still answer the other questions. That is, he might
say that momentary well-being is just a different ball game, and
that pure hedonism or some such theory provides the correct
account of momentary well-being, but that some correspondence
theory—desire satisfactionism, say—provides the correct account of

what makes a whole life go well, from a timeless perspective. Call this the *bifurcated view* of well-being.[58]

I think we should be skeptical of the bifurcated view. It lacks any obvious motivation other than to avoid problems about well-being and time. And it has some odd consequences. In addition to whole lives and moments, there are intermediate periods of time, such as adolescence. What sort of value do these intermediate periods have? Is it the sort of value that a whole life has, or the sort of value moments have? Neither answer is satisfactory. Consider first the view that intermediate periods of time have the sort of value whole lives have; their values are determined by such things as narrative structure or the satisfaction of goals or desires. This view has an unpalatable arbitrariness. It would seem arbitrary to calculate the value of a moment differently from the way we calculate the value of an intermediate interval.[59] If how well things are going for me *now* is determined by my *current* hedonic state, we should also say that how well things go for me for the next two seconds, or today, or this year, or during my adulthood, is similarly determined by my hedonic states during those times.

So let us suppose that an intermediate period of time has the same sort of value as a moment, and that a whole life has a different sort of value—a kind that is determined by features such as narrative structure and the achievement of goals. This view faces a similar problem. There are some very long intermediate periods of time. Consider the period of time that extends from my first moment of existence up until a second before I die. On the current proposal, the value of that period of time for me would be determined by my hedonic states during that time. What about the period of time that lasts my entire life? Surely that must also be determined by my hedonic states during that time. But then, on this proposal, the value of my life for me is not the same as the value for me of the period of time that stretches my entire life. That is a strange result as well.

---

[58] Velleman endorses a bifurcated view of well-being (1993, 345). I discuss further features of Velleman's view in Section 4.5. For a criticism of Velleman's view that is somewhat similar to my criticism of bifurcated views but draws the opposite moral, see McMahan 2002, 180.

[59] See McMahan 2002, 180.

Whether intermediate periods of time are evaluated like moments or like whole lives, we get unacceptable results. The bifurcated view is best avoided.

1.4 A Paradox

David Hume famously said, "'tis not contrary to reason to prefer the destruction of the whole world to the scratching of my finger ... 'Tis as little contrary to reason to prefer even my own acknowledg'd lesser good to my greater, and have a more ardent affection for the former than the latter."[60] Hume was surely wrong on the first count. But I think he was right on the second—at least, I think there may be some cases in which it is reasonable for someone to want to be badly off. If so then desire satisfactionism is paradoxical. And as we will see, this paradox extends to all correspondence theories. If a correspondence theory is true, there will be some cases in which a person's life goes well if and only if it does not go well. These are cases in which a person desires to be badly off, or takes pleasure in being badly off, or believes she is badly off.

I begin by formulating the paradox for each correspondence theory. To get a paradox for desire satisfactionism, we need a case where someone whose life is close to the threshold between good and bad desires his life to go badly. Suppose desire satisfactionism is true, and suppose Epimenides has just two desires. His first desire, D_a, is a desire of intensity $+5$ for an apple. He does not get the apple, so his life includes a desire frustration with a value of -5. His second desire, D_b, is a desire of intensity $+10$ that his life goes badly for him. Is D_b satisfied? If it is, then Epimenides' life contains a desire satisfaction of value $+10$, in which case his life has an overall value of $+5$ (it goes well for him), in which case D_b is not satisfied after all. If D_b is not satisfied, then his life contains a desire frustration of value -10, in which case his life has an overall value of -15 (it goes badly for him), in which case D_b is satisfied. Thus if desire satisfactionism is true, D_b is satisfied if and only if it is not satisfied, and Epimenides' life

---

[60] Hume 1978, II.III.III.

goes well if and only if it does not go well.[61] Desire satisfactionism is paradoxical.

This is a problem only if the life I have described for Epimenides is genuinely possible. Granted, it would be difficult for someone to have only two desires. But the life is described that way only to make the math easy; if you want a more complicated life, add more desire satisfactions and frustrations, so long as they balance out. If Epimenides' life is not possible as described, it must have something to do specifically with D_b. When someone reports having that desire, we might well find the person odd. We might want to know why they would have such a desire; we might suspect that they do not *really* desire to be badly off. But it certainly seems possible that someone could have it; in most cases, it does not create a paradox even if desire satisfactionism is true. And the mere possibility of having such a desire is what causes the problem. (I discuss some arguments for the claim that D_b is problematic below.)

Next consider truth-adjusted hedonism. Recall that according to truth-adjusted hedonism, the value of a pleasure is a function of its intensity and the truth-value of its object. Just to make things precise, suppose that pleasures taken in truths ('true pleasures') are twice as valuable as pleasures of similar intensity taken in falsehoods ('false pleasures'), so that a degree 10 pleasure has intrinsic value of +10 when it is taken in a false proposition, but +20 when it is taken in a true proposition. Suppose that Epimenides takes pleasure to degree 10 in the fact that his life is, on the whole, a bad one. Call this pleasure P. Suppose that there is only one other hedonic or doloric episode in Epimenides' life: an experience of pain with intrinsic value of −15. Is P a true pleasure or a false pleasure? If it is a true pleasure, then its intrinsic value is +20, which means his life has intrinsic value of +5, which means P is not a true pleasure after all. If P is a false pleasure, then P has intrinsic value of +10, which means his life has intrinsic value of −5, which means P was in fact a true pleasure. If truth-adjusted hedonism is true, then P is a true pleasure if and only if it is a false pleasure, and Epimenides' life is good if and only if it is bad. Truth-adjusted hedonism is paradoxical.

---

[61] For a nice statement of the paradox see Heathwood 2005, 502.

The paradoxes for true beliefism and achievementism work the same way. To get a paradox for achievementism, we just imagine a person whose achievement or project involves having his life go badly for him. Sometimes, that project or goal will be completed or achieved if and only if it is not completed or achieved. To get a paradox for true beliefism, we just imagine a person who believes that his life is going badly. Sometimes, his belief is true if and only if it is false, and his life is going badly if and only if it is not.

Note that this sort of paradox seems to arise only for correspondence theories. For example, according to pure hedonism, the value of a pleasure does not depend on the truth-value of its object; thus, there is no way to formulate an analogous paradox for pure hedonism.

The paradox itself is simple enough; the fun comes in talking about possible solutions. So now I turn to that. Before discussing attempts to avoid the paradox, I note that there are those who think the appropriate response to some paradoxes is to embrace true contradictions—in this case, to admit that there are some lives that are, in the same respect, both good and not-good.[62] I have nothing interesting to say about this response. Australian-rules logicians may wish to skip ahead.

1.4.1 *Worthiness*

The paradox might be avoided by rejecting Hume's striking claim and placing restrictions on the desire satisfactions, achievements or pleasures that make one's life go better. One might place a rationality or morality constraint on the intrinsic goods, so that only *rational* or *moral* pleasures, achievements, or desire satisfactions make one's life go better.[63] Feldman suggests that the value of a pleasure should be adjusted not only for the *truth* of its object, but also for its *pleasureworthiness*.[64] This view ('Desert-Adjusted Intrinsic Attitudinal Hedonism') might entail that the state of affairs consisting

---

[62] See, for example, Priest 1998 and 2004.

[63] Thanks to David Sobel for this suggestion; see Adams 1999, 84–93, and Carson 2000, ch. 3 for further discussion.

[64] Feldman 2004, 121.

of one's life going badly is undeserving of pleasure, and pleasures taken in that state of affairs might turn out to be worthless. As noted above, sophisticated desire satisfactionists and achievementists believe something similar about desires and achievements.[65]

This solution has no plausibility as a defense of true beliefism. The analogous move for true beliefism would be to distinguish belief-worthy from non-belief-worthy propositions, and to say that the belief that one's life is going badly is not belief-worthy. But it would seem that what makes a proposition belief-worthy is, at least in part, that it is true. If so, another paradox arises: a paradox of belief-worthiness. Very briefly: suppose A's life is going slightly badly, and suppose this fact bestows belief-worthiness on the proposition that A's life is going badly. Now, suppose A believes that proposition. Since A's belief is true, and (according to the proposed view) belief in a belief-worthy proposition makes A's life go better, A's life is pushed over the threshold, so that it is not going badly after all. So the proposition that A's life is going badly is not belief-worthy for A. If it is belief-worthy, then it is not. And so on, as before. The proposition that one's life is going badly will sometimes be belief-worthy if and only if it is false, and therefore not belief-worthy.

The worthiness solution is more promising as a defense of the other correspondence theories. But it requires the correspondence theorist to give an account of what distinguishes those states worthy of desire, pursuit, or pleasure from those that are unworthy—no small feat in itself. But suppose this can be done. The resulting account must be shown to entail that the objects of paradox-inducing desires, pleasures, and achievements are not worthy of desire, pleasure, or pursuit. It is not obvious that a plausible account of desire-worthiness would entail that one's life going badly is unworthy of desire. Suppose Jeff has performed some very bad actions, but has now developed a strong sense of justice. Jeff notices that when others perform the sorts of actions he performs, he desires that things go badly for them. He

---

[65] One might wonder why Feldman seems to be more sanguine about the prospects for an account of pleasure-worthiness than he is about the prospects for an account of desire-worthiness (compare Feldman 2004, 17, with Feldman 2004, 121–2).

realizes that he is relevantly like those other evildoers. Thus moral reflection leads him to desire that things go badly for him. We might judge him favorably for having such a desire; we might think he demonstrated an admirable sense of morality. We might also say Jeff is rational to have that desire—not that it is in his interest to have it, but that, in the broadest sense, he *ought* to have it.[66] The same may be said about taking pleasure in one's life going badly.

At this point the desire satisfactionist might appeal to a difference between 'intrinsic' and 'extrinsic' desires. To desire something intrinsically is to desire it for its own sake; to desire something extrinsically is to desire it for the sake of something else. Perhaps it is only the satisfaction or frustration of *intrinsic* desires that matters to welfare. Jeff's desire to have a bad life seems to be an extrinsic desire, since he desires a bad life only for the sake of justice, not for itself; thus, its satisfaction or frustration does not make Jeff's life better or worse.

This response merely relocates the problem. If Jeff's desire to have his life go badly is merely extrinsic since it is based on his desire for justice, then it will be his desire for justice that creates the paradox. Suppose Jeff's life goes badly. If, in virtue of his life going badly, his desire for justice is satisfied, then his life will contain an extra satisfaction, and therefore (given the appropriate stipulations, and contrary to our hypothesis) his life does not go badly after all. Paradox.

There is an option available to the achievementist that might not be available to the other correspondence theorists. We could say that it is irrational to pursue a goal that will be achieved if and only if it is not achieved.[67] In order to be rationally pursued, a goal must be possible to achieve. Pursuit of a goal may be unlike desire in this way; it may be entirely rational to *desire* something that cannot possibly obtain, but not rational (and perhaps not even possible) to *pursue* it.

But this is not a satisfactory reply. The goal of having one's life go badly is paradoxical, and hence impossible to achieve, *only if achievementism is true!* Pre-theoretically, it is an unproblematic (though

---

[66] This is in contrast to Darwall's self-loather, who seems irrational; see Darwall 2002, 5–6. For further discussion see Carson 2000, 90–1.

[67] Thanks to Doug Portmore for this suggestion.

unusual) goal. The irrationality of the goal, and the impossibility of pursuing it, cannot be established independently of the truth of the theory. So the solution is purchased at the cost of making paradoxical what seems unproblematic. (This problem mirrors the problem for Heathwood's response, which I discuss in more detail in Section 1.4.5.)

1.4.2 The hierarchical solution

One might say that it is only 'first-order' desire satisfactions, pleasures or beliefs that make one's life go better.[68] The desire satisfactionist might say that, since what make it true that one's life goes badly are facts about the satisfaction of one's desires, the desire for one's life to go badly is a 'second-order' desire—a desire about one's desires. Similarly, the pleasure one takes in living a bad life (not getting enough pleasure to outweigh one's pains) is a second-order pleasure, since it is a pleasure taken in facts about one's pleasures; the belief that one's life is going badly is a second-order belief, since it is a belief about one's beliefs.

But this is too quick; there is a complication about how the contents of propositional attitudes are individuated. If desire satisfactionism is true, but Epimenides does not believe that it is true, and desires his life to go badly, does Epimenides desire that his desires be frustrated? If not, the hierarchical solution is a non-starter, because the desire to have one's life go badly is not a second-order desire after all.[69] We can ignore this complication, however, because the hierarchical solution fails for independent reasons.

---

[68] Thanks to Jussi Suikkanen, Richard Chappell, Scott Wilson, and Campbell Brown for discussion of this idea.

[69] There is a related problem about how the hierarchical solution would work for true beliefism. Nobody thinks true beliefism is a complete theory of welfare, so it is not obvious that a belief that one's life is going badly is a second-order belief. Perhaps, ignoring the previous complication about individuating contents of propositional attitudes, the belief that one's life is going badly could be identified with the belief that the positive value of one's true beliefs, pleasures, and achievements is outweighed by the negative value of one's false beliefs, pains, and failures; perhaps such a belief counts as a second-order belief, since it is partly about one's beliefs.

Consider a smoker who desires to smoke, but also desires to be rid of the desire to smoke; when that second-order desire is satisfied, the desire satisfactionist should say that her life goes better. If she takes pleasure in the fact that she no longer gets pleasure from smoking, the hedonist should say that her life goes better in virtue of that second-order pleasure. Or consider someone who, after reading a lot of Epicurus, rids herself of most of her first-order desires; subsequently she regrets this, and desires to get some of those old desires back. If that second-order desire is satisfied, the desire satisfactionist should say that her life goes better. If she is pleased to be able to take pleasure in the satisfaction of those desires again, the hedonist should say that her life goes better in virtue of that second-order pleasure. We need some principled reason to say that such pleasures and desire-satisfactions are not valuable. It would be ad hoc for the defender of desire satisfactionism or truth-adjusted hedonism to deny their value simply to avoid paradox. Defenders of true beliefism ought to reject this move as well. It seems to curtail, arbitrarily, the intrinsic value of self-knowledge. Having an accurate self-conception, including true beliefs about the accuracy of one's own beliefs, seems like just the sort of thing a true beliefism defender ought to think makes one's life intrinsically better.

1.4.3 The anti-globality solution

Bertrand Russell once said, in introducing his theory of types, that 'whatever involves *all* of a collection must not be one of the collection.'[70] One might apply this idea to the paradox of welfare, and say that the paradox shows either (i) that there can be no truly 'global' desires (desires about one's *entire* life); or (ii) that satisfaction of such desires is not intrinsically good; or, most implausibly but following Russell's suggestion most closely, (iii) that global desires are not themselves part of one's life.

But this will not help either. Consider the following ridiculously simplified example. Suppose I live for two days, Tuesday and

---

[70] Russell 1971, 63.

Wednesday. Each day I have just one desire. On Tuesday, I have the following desire:

(D₁) The desire that my life does not go well on Wednesday.

On Wednesday, I have the following desire:

(D₂) The desire that my life goes well on Tuesday.

Neither D_1 nor D_2 is a global desire. Neither D_1 nor D_2 is paradoxical on its own; nor are they jointly paradoxical, unless desire satisfaction-ism is true. Suppose that desire satisfactionism is true. Is D_1 satisfied? If it is, then two things are true. (i) My life goes well on Tuesday, since I have just one desire on that day, and it is satisfied. (ii) My life does not go well on Wednesday, which means the one desire I have that day, D_2, is not satisfied. But if D_2 is not satisfied, then my life goes badly on Tuesday, in which case my Tuesday desire, D_1, must not be satisfied after all. So if my life goes well on Tuesday, then it does not. Suppose D_1 is not satisfied. Then two things are true. (i) My life does not go well on Tuesday, since D_1 is not satisfied. (ii) My life goes well on Wednesday, in which case D_2 is satisfied. But that means my life does go well on Tuesday after all. So if my life does not go well on Tuesday, then it does. So my life goes well on Tuesday if and only if it does not. We could construct similar examples, *mutatis mutandis*, for the other correspondence theories.

1.4.4 The liar-parasitic response

One might well be thinking something like the following: *This is a paradox of self-reference; it is just like the liar paradox, which is a problem for everybody. Why not just take the best solution to the liar and apply it, suitably modified, to the paradoxes for correspondence theories? Let the logicians solve the problem.*[71]

To be sure, the welfare and liar paradoxes have a similar self-referential flavor. Hence it is unsurprising that there are similarities between the Hierarchical and Anti-Globality solutions to the welfare

---

[71] JC Beall and an anonymous referee suggested something along these lines to me.

paradox and similar well-known solutions to the liar paradox. As we've seen, those solutions to the welfare paradox are not plausible. (Perhaps they are not plausible solutions to the liar paradox either.)

It cannot simply be assumed that a solution to the liar can be adapted to apply to the welfare paradox. Consider the view that liar sentences are self-contradictory. According to this view, an utterance of the liar sentence, 'This sentence is false,' implicitly asserts that it is true; so utterances of the liar sentence attribute both truth and falsity to themselves; so they are not paradoxical, but self-contradictory and therefore simply false.[72] Whatever the merits of this solution to the liar paradox, to adapt it to the welfare paradox would involve making the absurd claim that the desire to have one's life go badly somehow implicitly involves a desire to have one's life go well.

In general, there are good reasons to think the liar-parasitic strategy cannot be fully successful. In the case of the liar, there is obviously something defective or problematic about *the liar sentence itself* (or, in the case of the strengthened liar, about certain combinations of sentences taken together). The challenge is to say just *why* it is defective. But the corresponding item being evaluated here—desire/belief/pleasure/effort directed at one's own life going badly—does not seem inherently defective. We get a paradox only given the assumption that desire satisfactionism, truth-adjusted hedonism, achievementism, or true beliefism is the correct theory of welfare. Thus, we have good reason to wonder whether the paradox for correspondence theories is really so similar to the liar paradox after all.

1.4.5 Heathwood's response

Finally, there is the response given by Chris Heathwood. Heathwood defends only desire satisfactionism, but we will examine whether his solution generalizes to other correspondence theories. Heathwood attempts to get everyone else in the same boat as the desire satisfactionist:

---

[72] Prior 1961; Kirkham 1995, 294–5.

But not just desire-satisfaction theorists are mired in paradox. Analogous paradoxes get off the ground without assuming a desire theory of welfare. Imagine a person who desires, to intensity 10, that his net balance of desire satisfaction over frustration at some time be negative. Suppose he gets 6 units of desire frustration at that time. It would seem his balance is −6. But if it is, then his intensity 10 desire is satisfied, and so his net balance is +4. But then his intensity 10 desire is not satisfied. In short, this desire is satisfied if and only if it is not satisfied ... however the more basic paradoxes of desire are solved so will the paradoxes for desire-satisfaction theories be solved.[73]

The idea is that the paradox of desire arises independently of any theory of welfare; even if desire satisfactionism is not true, it is sometimes paradoxical for a person to desire that his desires be frustrated. So desire satisfactionism faces no *special* problem here.

Those who think true belief is intrinsically good might also employ Heathwood's strategy. Paradox can arise merely from the existence of a person who believes that most of his beliefs are false; at least sometimes, that belief is true if and only if it is false. Again, this is independent of any theory of welfare. The same goes for truth-adjusted hedonism. Suppose someone takes pleasure in the fact that most of his pleasures are false pleasures; at least sometimes, that pleasure is a true pleasure if and only if it is a false pleasure.[74] And the same goes for achievementism.

Heathwood's strategy seems more promising than the others we have seen. However, I think it must be rejected as well. Suppose that in order to avoid the paradox of desire, we must say that the desire to have one's desires be, on the whole, mostly frustrated, is at least sometimes impossible to have.[75] If desire satisfactionism were true, the impossibility of that desire would entail the impossibility of desiring one's life to go badly on the whole. But *that* desire does not seem impossible or paradoxical. A desire to have one's desires

---

[73] Heathwood 2005, 502–3.

[74] In Bradley 2007*b*, I claimed that Heathwood's strategy does not apply to TH. I was wrong. Thanks to Heathwood for cheerfully pointing out my error.

[75] Heathwood 2005, 502–3. Richard Chappell suggests a similar strategy for avoiding the paradox; see <http://pixnaps.blogspot.com/2005/02/this-desire-is-thwarted.html> and <http://pixnaps.blogspot.com/2005/02/is-immoral-value-possible.html>.

frustrated is transparently paradoxical; everyone must agree that such a desire is problematic in virtue of its self-referential quality. In this way, it is like the liar sentence. The desire to have one's life go badly is not like the liar sentence, nor is it like the desire to have one's desires frustrated. *It is not transparently paradoxical.* It seems like an unproblematic desire. It is paradoxical, and has liar-like features, only given a particular theory of welfare. So there's a cost to desire satisfactionism here—there is at least one desire that does not seem paradoxical, but in fact is paradoxical if, but *only* if, desire satisfactionism is true. The other correspondence theories pay the same price: prior to the adoption of a philosophical theory, it does not seem paradoxical to believe one's life is going badly, or take pleasure in it, or to pursue it, even if one's life is very close to the threshold between good and bad.

We have seen five responses to the paradox on behalf of correspondence theories. The hierarchical and anti-globality responses are entirely unsuccessful. The worthiness response is entirely unsuccessful as a defense of true beliefism. As a defense of achievementism, desire satisfactionism, or truth-adjusted hedonism, its plausibility depends on an account of the pursuit-, desire-, or pleasure-worthiness of propositions that entails that one's life going badly cannot be worthy of pursuit, desire, or pleasure. There are good reasons to be pessimistic about this. The liar-parasitic response seems unsatisfactory due to the fact that there is no reason to think that solutions to the liar can be adapted to the welfare paradox, and the fact that there seems to be nothing defective about the proposition that one's life is going badly, nor about the relevant desires, pursuits, pleasures, and beliefs. Finally, Heathwood's response seems unsatisfactory, since having a pro-attitude towards one's life going badly does not seem paradoxical independently of the assumption that some correspondence theory is the correct theory of welfare.

1.5 Conclusions and Implications

Correspondence theories have two serious problems: they cannot account for momentary well-being, and they are paradoxical. Perhaps the best the correspondence theorist can do is bite some bullets. He might just say that correspondence theories account only for lifetime well-being, and some other theory (pure hedonism?) must be employed to account for momentary well-being. But as we have seen, biting that bullet is very unappealing. He might say that the desire to be badly off or the belief that one is badly off really is paradoxical in some circumstances; hence, the Epimenides story does not describe a possible life. He might argue that, once we've accepted and internalized (e.g.) desire satisfactionism, the Epimenides story really does seem impossible (perhaps he would mention something about one philosopher's *modus tollens* being another's *modus ponens*).

Whether this is a reasonable response depends on whether correspondence theories are so attractive that it is best, all things considered, to bite these bullets. One might argue as follows: it is vitally important that a theory of welfare entail that a life on the experience machine is not a terrifically good life; only correspondence theories can yield this result; it is therefore worthwhile on the whole to endorse a correspondence theory, even if it requires us to say absurd things about momentary well-being and to say that it is impossible for someone living a mediocre life to desire (believe …) that his life go badly.

I think this defense of correspondence theories is dubious. We might wonder whether the problem with life on the experience machine is really the lack of mind–world correspondence. For it is not clear that correspondence theories do all that well, in general, at explaining what seems problematic about life on an experience machine. Consider someone who, while on the experience machine, takes pleasure only in her own sensations. If the pleasure is sufficiently intense, that person could have an outstanding life by the lights of truth-adjusted hedonism. Consider someone on the machine who desires only to have certain sensations, or attempts only to have nice sensations, or only has beliefs about his or her sensations; such a person could have a great life by the lights of desire satisfactionism, achievementism, or true beliefism, respectively. Furthermore, achievementists and true beliefists typically believe that pleasure is among the intrinsic goods; if so, then if one got enough pleasure, one could live a great life on the experience machine even without any achievement or true belief (though admittedly not as great as a similar life that had achievement or true belief in addition). Or imagine slightly different machines: for example, imagine a true belief machine, or a desire satisfaction machine, such that when you hook up to the machine it adjusts your beliefs or desires in such a way that they are all true or satisfied.[76] These machines seem just as problematic for true beliefists and desire satisfactionists as the experience machine is for hedonists. Since I believe I've shown that a price has been exacted from those who endorse correspondence theories, and the advantages of such theories with respect to experience machines are largely illusory, I think correspondence theories should be rejected.

If this is right, then having one's wishes ignored does not, in itself, constitute a harm. And this would of course apply to dead people as well. So the standard account of posthumous harm—that the dead can be harmed by having their wishes ignored—is false. Does this mean that there is no good reason to honor the wishes of the dead? Of course not. There are many other possible reasons. First, there could be welfare-based reasons to honor the wishes of the dead that are not based on attributing intrinsic value to the satisfaction of desires. For example, it could turn out that events happening after a person dies affect the story of the person's life for better or worse, and if the value of a person's life is determined by what sort of story it tells, as on the narrative structure view, those events could retroactively determine how well the life went. Second, there might be a Rossian prima facie duty to honor the wishes of the dead. This duty might be particularly strong for a person who has made a promise to honor those wishes. Such a duty is not based on the welfare of the deceased; it is not a duty of beneficence. Or it might be that failing to honor these wishes violates the *rights* of the deceased, without harming her—it is a harmless wrong. There are also indirect justifications for honoring the wishes of the dead. If people do not believe their wishes will be honored after they die, they will be likely to behave differently while alive. This could have bad consequences. Someone

[76] Thanks to Sören Häggqvist for this suggestion.

might think: 'I'd be happy to write a will leaving my millions to charity. But people do not honor the wishes of the dead, so I'd have no reason to think my will would be respected. I might as well just use the money to throw a decadent party and then burn what's left over on my deathbed.' I do not know how many people would think in this way, but it seems possible. Knowing that their wishes will not be honored after they die would also be likely to make people unhappy while they are alive. The reader can probably think of many other ways in which people would act and feel differently if they lived in a society where the wishes of the dead were seldom honored. This could provide a reason to have a society in which the wishes of the dead are respected (though, of course, it would not always provide a sufficient reason to respect the wishes of any particular dead person). I am inclined to think that the wishes of the dead are taken somewhat too seriously. But those who do take them seriously need not accept a correspondence theory of welfare, so long as they are satisfied with these other sorts of justifications.[77]

One might be thinking ahead to what is to come later in the book, and be puzzled. I am going to argue that *death* is bad for the one who dies. But I have just argued that *posthumous harm* is impossible. Is it possible to believe both of these things? Joel Feinberg says it is not: 'Either death and posthumous harms both alike can be harms, or neither can.'[78] But Feinberg says this only because he accepts a false view about the badness of death. Feinberg claims that death harms its victim *retroactively*, by making his life worse while he was alive and wanting various things that his death deprives

---

[77] For further discussion of posthumous harm and indirect justifications for respecting the wishes of the dead, see Callahan 1987; Taylor 2005, 320; and Kraut 2007, 261–3.

[78] Feinberg 1993, 174. Walter Glannon also maintains that the two positions go together; this seems to be because he thinks hedonists must deny that death is bad, and this in turn seems to be largely because he misunderstands the deprivation account of the badness of death. See Glannon 2001, especially p. 132, where he describes the deprivation account as the view, allegedly shared by Feldman and Nagel, that death is bad because it deprives its victim of extrinsic goods. No deprivation theorist believes this. See Ch. 2 for my formulation of the deprivation account.

him of.[79] This makes death just another sort of posthumous harm.
I deny that the harm of death is retroactive in this way, so death
and posthumous harm need not get the same treatment. There is
a crucial difference between death and posthumous harms. *Death*
makes an impact on its victim's well-being, by reducing it to zero,
but events happening *after* death do not—once a person has died,
his well-being level is stuck at zero forever, no matter what happens
afterwards.[80]

If we reject correspondence theories on the basis of the arguments
presented here, pure hedonism starts to look a lot more attractive.
But I cannot claim to have established the truth of pure hedonism.
I have not ruled out Feldman's desert-adjusted hedonism, though I
think this view has been shown to be problematic.[81] There are also
non-correspondence versions of desire satisfactionism: for example,
Heathwood's *subjective* desire satisfactionism, according to which
what is good for a person is that she thinks she gets what she wants.[82]
(Although desert-adjusted hedonism and subjective desire satisfactionism are not susceptible to my arguments, it should be noted that
neither view is compatible with the possibility of posthumous harm.)
Pure hedonism and Heathwood's subjective desire satisfactionism
entail that how well someone's life goes is determined entirely by
internal features of that life. But there are other, very different theories that might be untouched by the arguments of this chapter
as well, such as virtue-based theories. Whether such accounts of
well-being fall prey to the arguments given here depends on whether
virtue requires correspondence between mental states and the world.
Furthermore, I have not argued against 'holistic' axiologies such
as narrative structure views (Section 1.2.1), which cannot be understood as giving accounts of well-being-at-a-time. (I will argue in
Section 5.1 that such views are based on unreliable intuitions and lack
a convincing rationale.)

---

[79] Feinberg 1993, 184.

[80] Jens Johansson makes a similar point about the difference between the harm
of death and posthumous harms; see Johansson 2005, 98–9.

[81] See, for example, the ingenious argument in Lemos 2006.

[82] Heathwood, 'Subjective Desire Satisfactionism' (manuscript).

So the arguments I've given in this chapter do not establish pure hedonism, though they do raise doubts about some of its most popular competitors. However, even readers who are unconvinced by the arguments of this chapter should read on, since many of the arguments to come do not hinge on the success of the arguments given so far.

2

THE EVIL OF DEATH

See likewise of how little concern to us were the ages of eternal
time that passed before we were born. Nature holds this up to
us as a mirror of the time that will be after our death. Does this
appear in any way to be dreaded? Does it seem at all sad?

Lucretius[1]

2.1 Instrumental Value and Difference-Making

DEATH is typically bad for us in virtue of what it takes away from us.
It is instrumentally bad. To understand the badness of death, then,
we must understand instrumental value.

Some things are good or bad in virtue of causing intrinsically
good or bad things to happen. If Jack gives Will the toy from a
cereal box, his act causes Will some happiness, and the happiness is
intrinsically good. If Jack puts rocks in Will's cereal, Jack's action
causes Will to experience pain when he eats his cereal, and the pain
is intrinsically bad. Sometimes instrumental value has been defined
in the following way: something is instrumentally good if and only
if it causes something intrinsically good to happen; something is
instrumentally bad if and only if it causes something intrinsically bad
to happen.[2]

But many things are instrumentally good without causing anything
intrinsically good, and many things are instrumentally bad without

---

[1] Lucretius 1965, 110.   [2] See, for example, Baylis 1958, 488.

causing anything intrinsically bad. These are goods and evils of *prevention*. If Jack receives a vaccination that prevents him from contracting a painful illness, the vaccination is instrumentally good for Jack, even if it does not cause him any enjoyment. Likewise, if Jack intercepts some money intended for Will without Will ever finding out about it, and the money would have made Will happy, Jack's action is instrumentally bad for Will, even though nothing intrinsically bad happens to Will as a result of the action. The badness of death is relevantly like this, only much more severe; it deprives us of all possibility of future intrinsic goods.

At bottom, Jack's putting rocks in Will's cereal and Jack's secretly stealing Will's money are bad for Will in the same way: *they make things worse for Will than they would have been otherwise.* They do this in different ways, but the net result is the same. So in order to see these actions as bad, and to determine how bad they are, we must see *what difference they make* to the value of Will's life. This involves comparing how things go for Will with how things would have gone if the actions had not been done. If Jack had not stolen the money, or put the rocks in the cereal, Will would have had a happier life.

Instrumental value is not the only kind of value that has this feature. Intrinsic value has it too. When something is intrinsically good for someone, its obtaining makes things go better for that person than they would have gone otherwise. There is one difference, however: the extent of something's intrinsic goodness or badness is not determined by any comparison with what would have happened. It is determined by the intrinsic features of the intrinsically good or bad state.

It will be useful to focus our discussion on a single value that combines intrinsic and instrumental value: call this *overall value*. The overall value of something for a person is the difference it makes to how things go for that person, taking into account both its intrinsic and instrumental value (and whatever other sorts of value it has). Henceforth when I talk about the value of something I should be understood as talking about its overall value unless I say otherwise.

Since the value of an event is to be understood by appeal to what would have happened if it had not obtained, we have to understand counterfactual conditionals, or statements of the form: if X were to have happened, Y would have happened. A popular way to interpret such conditionals, due to David Lewis and Robert Stalnaker, employs the notion of *possible worlds*.[3] According to this view, to say that if X were to have happened, Y would have happened, is to say that at the closest possible world in which X happens, Y happens. Let us follow Lewis in thinking of closeness in terms of similarity; one world is closer to the actual world than another just in case it is more similar.[4]

The nature of possible worlds is disputed, but such disputes need not concern us. Let us think of a possible world as a complete story about the universe: a maximal consistent set of propositions. There is one such story corresponding to the actual world; the story it tells is the story of the actual history of our whole universe from beginning to end. But there are many alternative stories. Some of these are similar to the actual story in certain respects. The most similar world where X does not happen must differ from ours not only with respect to whether X happens, but also with respect to the *consequences* of X's happening or not. The closest world where Oswald does not shoot JFK is not a world that goes on like our world after the time of the shooting; it is not a world where, after proceeding along in the motorcade and not getting shot, JFK is suddenly dying of a devastating head wound even though nobody shot him. That world would be very different in an important way, since it would be a world where people get devastating head wounds for absolutely no reason—a world fundamentally unlike ours. Rather, the closest world is a world where he proceeds along in the motorcade waving to the spectators ... (and alternative historians tell us what happens after that). So to consider what would have happened had one actual event not happened is to consider a world where a great many things are different from the actual world.

What counts as the most similar world to the actual world is not always a determinate matter. It depends on what features of the actual world we want to keep fixed, or on what similarity relation we are employing. Must the most similar world where event E does not occur be a world just like the actual world right up until the time of E? Or can it be different at times before E? Consider this example:

---

[3] See Lewis 1973, and Stalnaker 1984.   [4] Lewis 1986a, 20–7.

a woman dies of cancer at time t after a year-long struggle. What is the most similar world where she does not die at time t? We might say it is a world where she dies the next day. Or we might say it is a world where she did not get cancer a year ago, or where her cancer had gone into remission, or where she had been completely cured. The first answer is the one we most likely get if we suppose the past must remain fixed. The others are answers we might get if we allow the past to vary. We cannot get a determinate answer to the question 'what would have happened?' until we decide what must remain fixed and what may vary.

Returning to value, the idea is that the value of some event for a person depends on the difference it makes to how things go for that person. To determine this, we look at how well things actually go for the person, and compare that with how well they would have gone had that event not happened. Given the interpretation of counterfactuals we are employing, this means that we must compare how well things go for the person with how well they go at the most similar world at which the event does not occur. And given that there are many similarity relations, we must relativize the value of an event to a similarity relation. Following the terminology introduced in Section 1.2.1, let us say that the extent to which things go well or badly for a person S at a world w is *the intrinsic value of w for S*. This gives us the following view, the **Difference-Making Principle**, which is very similar to views defended by Fred Feldman and John Broome:[5]

> **DMP**. The value of event E, for person S, at world w, relative to similarity relation R = the intrinsic value of w for S, minus the intrinsic value for S of the most R-similar world to w where E does not occur.

DMP entails that, when death takes a good life from its victim, that person's death is bad. Conversely, it entails that when death keeps a person from living a bad life, it is good for that person. It also gives us an extent to which death is good or bad: the more of a good life it takes away, the worse it is; the more of a bad life it takes away, the better it is. These are intuitively *the right answers* to the

---

[5] Feldman 1991; Broome 1999.

questions: under what circumstances is death bad, and when it is bad, how bad is it? Moreover, it gets those right answers by embodying a general idea that is *intuitively plausible*: that the value of something for me depends on *what difference it makes* to how things go for me. These are good features of DMP. DMP also has other features I like. It is a *simple* and *elegant* view. Simple and elegant views are to be preferred over complicated, convoluted, and ugly views. DMP has no ad hoc features or ugly asymmetries obviously designed to account for a small number of problem cases; the formulation flows directly from the attempt to capture the difference-making idea. And DMP does not presuppose any particular theory of what is intrinsically valuable, so it is *flexible*. It accounts for the badness of death without appealing, for example, to the idea that it is intrinsically bad to have one's desires frustrated.[6] It gives right answers; it is based on an intuitively plausible idea; it is simple and elegant; it is flexible. These are all good reasons to accept DMP.

One might worry about the relativization to similarity relations. DMP seems to entail that whether an event counts as good or bad can depend in part on features of conversational context, since it is context that picks out a similarity relation. As Alastair Norcross says about acts, 'sometimes different, equally normal contexts can render one act a harming or a benefiting.'[7] This is fishy. Someone might argue in this way: linguistic contexts do not determine the real, objective features of the world; harms and evils are real, objective features of the world; so linguistic context cannot make an event bad. Surely I cannot render an event bad just by getting myself into a certain linguistic context, as Norcross (perhaps unintentionally) suggests. Perhaps I can render certain *statements* about harms or evils true by shifting contexts, but that is not the same as making an event bad.

But this argument misunderstands the role of context with respect to DMP. DMP is an account of *value*, not an account of *value-claims*. Conversational context does indeed pick out a similarity relation. But

---

[6] This is in contrast to Nagel 1979 and others. Walter Glannon (2001, 132) claims that the deprivation account (and hence, I assume, DMP) is incompatible with hedonism, but only because he misunderstands the deprivation account (see Ch. 1 note 78).

[7] Norcross 2005, 168.

this does not mean that context determines whether an event is bad or not. Conversational context also picks out events to be evaluated, and people for whom we are determining whether the events are good or bad; this does not mean that whether that event is bad for that person depends in any way on context. The role of context, contrary to what an uncharitable reading of Norcross's statement suggests, is merely to pick out, among the real events, people, and similarity relations in the world, which one(s) we are talking about. Once that choice is made, *it is not up to us* whether that event is good or bad for that person relative to that similarity relation.

This might not entirely alleviate worries about relativizing to similarity relations. One might think that among the similarity relations, *only one* is relevant to questions about instrumental goodness and badness; certain sorts of facts are special, and must always be held fixed. I am skeptical of this notion, for reasons that will emerge in the rest of this chapter and in Chapter 5. But the existence of such a special similarity relation would not significantly affect the conclusions that follow. In fact, if it could be shown that there is such a special similarity relation, some of the problems I deal with in this book would disappear altogether. It is only with reluctance that I conclude that no similarity relation is special; I would be happy to be convinced otherwise.

In the remainder of this chapter I will discuss some cases that some have found problematic for DMP. Discussion of these cases will help show exactly what we are committed to if we endorse DMP, and what moves are available to the DMP-defender. I will show that these cases are not as problematic for DMP as some have supposed. But I will also present close relatives of DMP that some might prefer.

2.2 Overdetermination, Preemption, and Causation

DMP seems to face problems involving overdetermination and preemption.[8] Jeff McMahan provides a good example:

---

[8] The problems described here mirror problems for counterfactual analyses of causation. See Schaffer 2000 for a discussion of these problems.

The Young Pedestrian. A young man, aged twenty, absentmindedly steps off the curb into the path of a bus and is instantly and painlessly killed. During the autopsy, it is discovered that he had a hitherto silent cerebral aneurysm that would inevitably have burst within a week if he had not been hit by the bus. And the bursting of the aneurysm would certainly have been fatal.[9]

DMP seems to entail that the Young Pedestrian's death was not very bad for him, since it deprived him of very little life. This seems like an implausible result.[10] Of course, the case of the Young Pedestrian differs only in degree from every other death. Every death preempts some later death. It's just that in this particular case, the preempted death would have occurred soon after the time of the actual death, and both the actual death and the preempted death seem tragically premature.

Things are not so clear when we remember that there are many similarity relations. This provides us with the flexibility to account for these cases in such a way that the evaluation of a death rides piggy-back on a determination of the closest possible world. What is the most similar possible world in which the Young Pedestrian does not die at t_1? Typically, it is a world in which the past as of t_1 (or shortly before t_1) is completely similar to the actual past as of t_1, so that if he had not died at t_1, he would still have died of an aneurysm shortly after t_1 anyway.[11] To suppose that he would not have had an aneurysm in the first place would be to make a gratuitous historical change. But such a change is not *always* gratuitous. To illustrate, consider two obvious answers we might give to a question about the Young Pedestrian's death:

'Was the Young Pedestrian's death at t_1 bad?'

ANSWER #1: *Yes, very bad. He was a young man at t_1. He would have been better off dying at a much later time.*

---

[9] McMahan 2002, 117.

[10] Elizabeth Harman raised a similar objection in her comments on Bradley 2004 at the Bellingham Summer Philosophy Conference. This is what McMahan calls 'The Metaphysical Problem' for the Token Comparison View, which is essentially the view I defend here (McMahan 2002, 107); see McMahan 1988; Feldman 1991; and Feit 2002 for further discussion of this problem.

[11] Cf. Lewis 1979.

ANSWER #2: *Yes, but not very bad, because he would have died within a week anyway from a burst aneurysm.*

Either of these answers (and probably many others) could be correct, depending on the context. We would typically give ANSWER #1. When we find out about the aneurysm, our answer might change to ANSWER #2; but even when we know about the aneurysm, we may still feel a strong pull to ANSWER #1. I think the reason is that we are pulled in different directions by different resolutions of the vagueness of the question, and we have different comparisons in mind at the same time, corresponding to different similarity relations.

What world is the most similar world where the Young Pedestrian does not die at t1? Sometimes it is a world where he dies only a week later; but sometimes the nearest world must be one in which he dies at a time long after t1, even if that makes certain 'backtracking' counterfactuals come out true (e.g., if he had not died at t1, he would not have had an aneurysm before t1).[12] ANSWER #2 seems right if we are asking 'was the Young Pedestrian's death at t1, by being hit by a bus, given that he had an aneurysm, bad for him?' In such a context, we have in mind a similarity relation that counts facts about the very recent past as very important in determining overall similarity. As Lewis says, 'facts just mentioned may have a special claim to be held fixed.'[13] On the other hand, ANSWER #1 seems right if we are asking 'was it bad for him to die at t1, rather than in old age?'[14] In this context, we have in mind a similarity relation that does not count facts about the recent past as important. The question itself directs us to look for the closest world where he dies much later. Different ways of asking the question make different answers turn out to be correct; the additions to the question help to clarify what similarity relation is being employed. The way of asking the question

---

[12] Lewis 1979.   [13] Lewis 1986a, 21.

[14] We might wish to take the 'rather than' clause even more seriously. We might say that what is good or bad for someone is not the occurrence of some event E, but the occurrence of E *rather than some alternative E**. This would result in an explicitly contrastivist view analogous to Jonathan Schaffer's contrastive account of causation (Schaffer 2005). I will not develop the account here, since I am not convinced it would really be any better than DMP. Thanks to Jens Johansson for discussion of this point.

that favors Answer #2 emphasizes the *cause* of death; the way that favors Answer #1 emphasizes its *timing*. We are led to think there is a problem in the case of the Young Pedestrian because the example emphasizes details concerning the cause of death. But the cause of the death is typically much less important in the evaluation of the death than its timing; the timing is what determines (in conjunction with other obvious facts) how bad someone's death is.[15] Thus we often do not care to keep the recent past fixed when determining which world is most similar, since doing so seems to require keeping cause of death fixed too.

Of course, even once we have focused on the timing of the death, different answers may be correct depending on whether we want to know whether death at *precisely* t₁ was bad for the Young Pedestrian or whether death at *roughly* t₁ was bad for him. Consider the following answer to the question:

Answer #3: *The Young Pedestrian's death* at t₁ *was not bad at all. If he had not died at precisely t₁, he would have died a millisecond later or earlier. That would not have made a difference. There is nothing special about t₁ that makes it a bad time to die.*

Usually it is not permissible to count a world where he dies a millisecond after t₁ as the closest world where he does not die at t₁, as illustrated by the oddness of Answer #3.[16] Though Answer #3 seems strange, it should be clear that a world in which he gets hit by a bus at t₁-plus-one-millisecond is more similar to the actual world in certain respects than one in which the bus does not hit him at all. This seems to favor Answer #3 over #1 or #2. A context in which Answer #3 makes sense is one in which it is asked 'was the Young Pedestrian's death at t₁ (rather than any other time, such as a millisecond earlier or later) bad for him?' The reason Answer #3 seems odd is that we do not usually interpret the question in this way. While we are usually interested in the timing of a death for the purposes of evaluating it,

---

[15] Feit discusses, but does not endorse or reject, a strategy like this (Feit 2002, 379–80). He views it as an alternative to Feldman's view, but I think it is consistent with Feldman's view, and may help to defend Feldman's view against McMahan's charge that it is ad hoc (McMahan 2002, 119–20).

[16] See Lewis 2000, 190.

we are not interested in the time because of anything having to do with *the time itself*; we are interested in the time only because we want to know how much of a good life has been taken from the deceased. That is, when evaluating an actual death that occurs at time t, we do not wish to employ a similarity relation that counts a world as more similar if an event just like that death happens at a time very close to t.

Another reason ANSWER #3 seems odd is that it presupposes the modal fragility of deaths. That is, it presupposes that if things had gone even the slightest bit differently—if he had died just a millisecond later—then we'd have a different death. But events generally, and deaths in particular, do not seem to be modally fragile in this way. We talk about events in much the same way we talk about objects and people. Just as we say that a table might have been a different color, or that a person might have been shorter, we also say that a death might have occurred earlier or later. If so, then the closest world where the Young Pedestrian's actual death does not occur will not be one where he dies in an extremely similar way, from the same cause, a millisecond later. When we think of such a world, we are really thinking of a world where the *very same death* occurs, but at a different time.

Even if I have shown that DMP can account for the claim that was initially supposed to be correct—that the Young Pedestrian's death was very bad for him—some will be unsatisfied. DMP accounts for not only that claim, but also the apparently implausible claim that the Young Pedestrian's death was not very bad for him, since ANSWER #2 is sometimes acceptable. The commitment to multiple answers to the question of how bad his death was for him might seem problematic, but I do not think so. It provides the best explanation of the fact that we are pulled in different directions by the example. Any theory that entails that his death is very bad for him absolutely, and *requires* us to compare his death with a much later possible death, does violence to a conflicting intuition: namely, that it was not so bad that he died when he did, *given that he had an aneurysm*. When the aneurysm is emphasized, I do feel a strong inclination to say that his actual death by bus was not all that bad for him. The emphasis on the aneurysm makes one sort of similarity relation more salient. But I also feel a pull to say the opposite, because it is natural to focus on the time of the death rather than its cause. The relativity to similarity relations provides an explanation for the conflicting pulls.

The solution to the preemption problem I advocate here is similar to the one advocated by Feldman.[17] According to Feldman, what we evaluate are states of affairs involving a person's death; and there are many such states of affairs that obtain when the Young Pedestrian dies. Among them are:

YPt. The young pedestrian dies at time t.

YPb. The young pedestrian is hit by a bus.

YPy. The young pedestrian dies in his youth.

Each of these states of affairs must be evaluated individually. The closest world where YPt does not obtain seems to be one where he dies just before or after t; thus, YPt is not bad at all for him. The closest world where YPb does not obtain is likely one where he dies of an aneurysm a week later; so YPb is not very bad for him. The closest world where YPy does not obtain is one where he lives a much longer life; so YPy is very bad for him. When we evaluate the Young Pedestrian's death, we are really evaluating one of these states of affairs. Whether we think his death is bad for him depends on which of these states of affairs we mean to evaluate.

McMahan finds Feldman's account unacceptable, for two reasons. First, he complains that Feldman has changed the subject; rather than evaluating the actual concrete event of the Young Pedestrian's death, Feldman is evaluating 'a certain type of event—death while young.'[18] I think this criticism is not entirely fair, because Feldman does not seem to believe in concrete events—at least he does not formulate his view in terms of events. All talk about events, in Feldman's discussions, is translated into talk about states of affairs or propositions.[19] So it is no surprise that Feldman does not evaluate the *event* of the Young Pedestrian's death. But we might then have the following worry: Feldman's account of overdetermination cases makes sense only given an ontology of states of affairs, not for an ontology of events. It would be better to have an account that is

[17] Feldman 1991, 224–6.   [18] McMahan 2002, 120.   [19] Feldman 1991, 212.

compatible with the existence of concrete events, and provides for the evaluation of such things.

This is precisely what DMP provides. McMahan cannot complain that DMP changes the subject. DMP tells us how to determine the value of a particular, concrete event: the Young Pedestrian's death. Of course, it does not provide for a *univocal* evaluation of that event, since the evaluation is relative to a similarity relation.

McMahan's deeper complaint is that Feldman's response is ad hoc.

There seems to be no principled reason why the death should be compared with the closest alternative in which the victim does not die young rather than, for example, the closest alternative in which he does not die prematurely, or in which he does not die before reaching old age, or in which he does not die before attaining the maximum human life span, or in which he does not die at all.[20]

What McMahan says is true, but it is not an objection to Feldman's view, or to mine. There are many distinct states of affairs related to the Young Pedestrian's death, any of which we might be interested in evaluating. Feldman suggests that we may wish to evaluate the state of affairs consisting of the Young Pedestrian dying young. The closest world at which he does not die young is one in which he dies in old age—not one where he does not die, or where he reaches the maximum human life span. This is not arbitrary, because a world where he dies in old age is more similar to the actual world than one where he does not die at all or where he reaches the maximum life span. A world in which he does not die at all involves a gratuitous change from the actual world: a change in the laws of nature, or the intervention of some divine being, or the invention of an immortality potion.

Perhaps McMahan's objection is to Feldman's choice of YPy as the state of affairs that is the Young Pedestrian's misfortune. But we might also wish to evaluate a different state of affairs:

YPd. YP dies.

The nearest world at which YPd does not obtain is one where he lives forever. So YPd may be very bad for the Young Pedestrian,

---

[20] McMahan 2002, 120.

depending on how his immortal life would go for him. There is no arbitrariness to Feldman's view, because Feldman does not choose YPy as the sole death-related state of affairs that is bad for the Young Pedestrian. There are many others, including YPd. It is not clear why this should be a problem.

McMahan's arbitrariness charge does not apply to DMP either. On Feldman's view, there are many states of affairs relating to the Young Pedestrian's death that are bad for him; similarly, according to DMP, there are many similarity relations such that his death is bad for him relative to that similarity relation. Choosing one of these relations as being in some way special might be arbitrary, but I have not suggested that we choose.

Those who find relativity to similarity relations unsatisfactory might wish to divorce causation from counterfactuals, and say that the Young Pedestrian's actual death at t₁ *causes* him to miss out on many years of life even though the closest world where he does not die at t₁ is a world where he dies shortly afterwards. According to this line of reasoning, the existence of the aneurysm does not prevent us from saying that the bus accident caused him to miss out on years of life. If the bus had not hit him, the aneurysm *would* have caused him to miss out on years of life; but that does not prevent us from saying that the bus accident *actually* caused him to miss out on those years. This is apparently to deny that *causes are difference-makers*, or at least to deny that C's causing E entails that C makes a difference to whether E occurs.[21] Since the bus accident does not make a difference to whether the Young Pedestrian lives to a ripe old age, if we are to claim that it causes him not to live to a ripe old age, we must deny that causes are difference-makers.

It is questionable whether causal judgments are any less context-sensitive than judgments about difference-making.[22] However, it may be useful to formulate a close relative of DMP that appeals to causality rather than counterfactuals. We simply need to distinguish those states of affairs that a death *causes* to obtain from those that

[21] On causation and difference-making see, for example, Lewis 1986*b*.

[22] For a recent argument that causal judgments are context-sensitive, see Hall 2007, 126–7.

it causes *not* to obtain. In the example of the Young Pedestrian, his death at t₁ causes certain states of affairs to obtain (such as the state *that he has no experiences at t₁-plus-ten-years*), and causes other states not to obtain (such as *that he is happy at t₁-plus-ten-years*). Call the conjunction of all states of affairs that an event causes to obtain the *total consequence* of the event; call the conjunction of all states of affairs that an event causes not to obtain the *total prevention* of the event. We could then formulate an explicitly **Causal Principle of Value** as follows:

> **CPV.** The value of an event for an individual = the intrinsic value for that individual of the total consequence of the event, minus the intrinsic value for that individual of the total prevention of the event.[23]

CPV entails that the Young Pedestrian's death is very bad for him, provided that the bus accident caused him to miss out on many years of valuable life. Some may find CPV to be an improvement over DMP. In Section 2.5 I will argue for DMP over CPV, in light of the fact that CPV, insofar as it differs from DMP, abandons the difference-maker idea. This makes little difference to what follows, but has some relevance to what happens in Chapter 5.

2.3 Genuine Evils, Fitting Attitudes, and the Symmetry Problem

Kai Draper argues that something might count as bad for me according to DMP without being a genuine evil.[24] DMP gives an account of comparative evil, but does not give an account of the sorts of evils worth caring about. For example, *not finding Aladdin's lamp* is comparatively bad for me—I would have been better off if I had

---

[23] Earl Conee proposes a rough sketch of a view along these lines; see Conee 2006, 183–5.

[24] Draper 1999. For a more thorough discussion of Draper's examples see Feit 2002.

found it—but it is not a genuine evil, since it does not merit any negative feelings.[25] Thus I have not shown that we should worry at all about the evil of death. Perhaps death, though worse for us than continued life, is nevertheless 'nothing to us,' as Epicurus says.

It is important to distinguish between the value of something and the appropriateness of having certain feelings or attitudes about that thing. There are a great many bad things happening in the world right now. Anyone who felt bad about all these things would be unbearably miserable all the time. There would be something wrong with such a person; his attitudes would be, in an important way, inappropriate.

I am interested here in the value of death, not so much in how people should feel about it. I have presented a view according to which death is bad for its victim. According to this view, not finding Aladdin's lamp is bad for someone too. And I think this result is correct. To be sure, there would be something odd about a person who got very upset about the fact that he has not yet found Aladdin's lamp. But this merely shows that there are things that are bad for us that we should not worry about very much.

Here it is useful to make a distinction between what emotional response a misfortune *merits* and what it is all-things-considered rational to feel about it. No doubt it is all-things-considered irrational to bemoan the fact that one has not found Aladdin's lamp. But it is also all-things-considered irrational to feel constantly despondent over the millions of deaths suffered by people each year. Anyone who did would be emotionally crippled. This does not show that those deaths do not *merit* any bad feelings. Each of those deaths merits a great deal of bad feeling. I say that the fact that I have not found Aladdin's lamp is very bad for me indeed, and *merits* bad feelings, but nevertheless it is irrational for me to feel bad about it at all, even a little bit. There is no necessary connection between the value of something and the all-things-considered rationality of having some feeling about it. There is a connection, but it is defeasible. I expect that the story about the conditions of defeat will be messy and unsystematic, involving facts about spatiotemporal proximity and personal relationships, among other things.

My death also merits bad feelings. And it seems to me that my death is unlike Aladdin's lamp, in that it is rational to feel bad about my future death but not about my failure to find Aladdin's lamp. However, it is very hard to say where the difference lies. Perhaps it has to do with the fact that I have some control over when my death occurs.[26] But if I am suffering from a terminal, incurable disease, and am paralyzed, I might have no control over the timing of my death, yet it still seems rational to feel bad about it.[27] Or perhaps the difference has to do with the fact that unlike not finding Aladdin's lamp, my death deprives me of things that I would be reasonable in expecting to get, as Draper suggests. But this is not clear, for it might be rational to feel bad about not getting something that is unreasonable to expect; for example, it might be rational for me to feel bad about the fact that I will one day die, even though it would not be reasonable to expect immortality.[28] Perhaps there is no important difference between dying and not finding Aladdin's lamp. If that is so, and if we should not feel bad about not finding Aladdin's lamp, then Epicurus was right: we should not feel bad about death at all. Fearing death is irrational. But death is still bad for us, and it is still generally rational to take steps to avoid it when such steps are available (just as it would be rational to take steps to find Aladdin's lamp, if only it existed!), and this is more important than what attitude we should have towards it.[29]

Being careful to distinguish the badness of something from the rationality of feeling bad about it also helps to make sense of Lucretius' 'symmetry problem.' We feel bad at the prospect of dying, and especially dying too young; but we do not feel bad at all about having been born later than we could have been.[30] We might take this to be a problem for DMP. If our feelings of fear are indicators of value,

---

[26] See Johansson 2005, 128–9.
[27] Nagel makes a similar point about inevitability; see Nagel 1979, 10.
[28] Thanks to Chris Heathwood for discussion here.
[29] For a defense of the rationality of fearing death, see Murphy 1976.
[30] Lucretius 1965, 110.

and we fear early death but not late birth, then it seems it is worse to die early than to be born late.[31]

As Feldman points out, in some cases the difference in badness can be explained by appeal to an asymmetry in the evaluations of the relevant counterfactuals. When someone dies young, it is normally the case that the person would have lived a longer life had she not died then; so DMP entails that her death is bad for her. But late birth does not normally involve a shorter life span; it is not bad to be born in 1971 rather than 1961 (assuming this is even possible), because being born in 1971 rather than 1961 seems to involve (say) dying in 2051 rather than 2041.[32] So DMP normally does not entail that late birth is bad.

But we can imagine cases where one's date of death should be held fixed. In such cases, DMP will entail that late birth is bad. Frederik Kaufman argues that this is a bad result for the view.

One's death might not deprive at all, whereas one's birth could deprive one of much, implying that one's birth was a terrible tragedy and one's death is value-neutral .... Apparently, then, one could lead a full and happy life oblivious to the terrible tragedy that occurred by being born. Something has gone wrong with the deprivation account if it entails that one's birth could be a terrible tragedy and one's death not bad at all.[33]

Kaufman's argument is misleading. The tragedy is not the birth, but its *lateness*. Here we should note another asymmetry in our evaluations of births and deaths. When we say that a person's death was a misfortune for her, we normally mean that it was worse than a later death; thus we compare the actual world to a world where she dies later, rather than to a world where she does not die at all. When we say that a person's birth was a misfortune, we normally mean that the person would have been better off never having been born; thus we normally compare the actual world to a world where she was never born, rather than to a world where she was born earlier (or later). So the question at issue here is: is it bad for a person

---

[31] For an excellent overview and discussion of the symmetry problem see ch. 5 of Johansson 2005.

[32] See Feldman 1991, 221–3, and Johansson 2005, 108.   [33] Kaufman 2004, 253.

to have been born late, if this makes the person's life go worse on the whole?

I think the answer to this is clearly 'yes.' Chris Belshaw gives a nice example that makes this answer seem plausible.[34] Suppose that I originated from an embryo that was formed in 1961. Scientists gave my parents a choice: either implant the embryo now, or freeze the embryo and wait ten years. My parents believed that, as a result of improved medical technology and the like, life was getting better and better for people, and would continue to do so for the foreseeable future. So they decided to wait to implant the embryo, in hopes that my life would go better as a result; thus I was born in 1971 rather than 1961. Suppose also that an asteroid collision will destroy all life on earth next year. It seems clear to me that in light of the asteroid collision, my parents, despite their best intentions, made the wrong decision. They might well regret their decision to wait, and would be rational to do so. So there is no counterexample to DMP, because it seems right in this case to say that my late birth is bad for me.[35]

Of course, even if my late birth were bad for me, my feelings about it would be very different from my feelings about my early death. I dread early death; it makes me worry. But even if I knew I missed out on ten years of life at the beginning of my life by being born late, I would not dread the missed time. In fact I would hardly care about it at all. The good life my late birth deprived me of would be past by now anyway, and like everyone else, I am *biased towards the future*. I care more about future goods and evils than past ones.[36] I want my goods to be in the future; I do not want bad things to be in my future; I do not care so much about whether I have goods and evils in my past. I do not know whether this bias is rational or not.[37]

---

[34] Belshaw 2000, 74–8.

[35] Note that this is still not quite the sort of case Kaufman had in mind, since he wanted a case where late birth is a deprivation but death is not. In my example, my death is still bad for me. In order to get the sort of case Kaufman wants, we'd have to insert a second catastrophe, like a devastating plague that immediately precedes the asteroid collision. I take it this does not matter to the evaluation of the case.

[36] Parfit 1984, ch. 8.

[37] Feldman claims that the bias is irrational; see Feldman 1991, 223.

But even if it is, it does not mean that late birth is not bad. If the bias to the future is rational, then sometimes, even though something is bad for me, it is irrational for me to feel very bad about it, because it's in the past.

This does not mean that I need to take a stand on the truth of currently popular 'fitting attitude' analyses of value.[38] According to such analyses, for something to be good (bad) just is for it to be fitting, or appropriate, or rational, to have some pro- (con-) attitude towards that thing. For reasons already given, this analysis of value is obviously false if 'rational' is taken in the all-things-considered sense that includes pragmatic reasons to have attitudes towards things. Circumstances might dictate that it is irrational or inappropriate to have a pro-attitude towards something that, in and of itself, merits a pro-attitude, for having that pro-attitude might lead to misery. But if 'rational' is taken in a more restricted sense, or in a prima facie, defeasible sense, some analysis along these lines might well be true.

2.4 Harm

DMP is a view about the values of events. It tells us under what conditions an event is *bad for* someone. Closely related to the concept of badness is the concept of *harm*. I am inclined to say that something is bad for a person if and only if it harms her; thus, an event harms a person if and only if it makes things go worse for that person than they would have gone otherwise. Call this account of harm the **Difference-Making Principle of Harm**, or DMPH.[39] But there seem to be instances where a person is harmed without being made

---

[38] For recent discussions, see Scanlon 1998; Rabinowicz and Rønnow-Rasmussen 2004; Olson 2004*b*; and Vayrynen 2006, among many others.

[39] DMPH is the most natural way to interpret Derek Parfit's much-discussed consequentialist account of harm; see Parfit 1984, 69. Parfit notes that on the ordinary use of the word 'benefit,' it is possible to benefit someone without making her better off; it's clear he thinks the corresponding thing about the ordinary use of 'harm.' On my view, what Parfit calls the 'ordinary' use of 'harm' picks out the concept of prima facie harm.

worse-off. James Woodward discusses several such cases,[40] and more recently Elizabeth Harman discusses some similar cases:

Rape: A woman is raped, becomes pregnant, and ends up raising the child .... The woman's life is better, due to the value of her relationship with her child, than it would have been if she had not been raped, even taking into account the trauma of the rape.

Nazi Prisoner: A man was imprisoned in a Nazi concentration camp ... his experience in the camp enriched his character and deepened his understanding of life, such that overall his life was better than it would have been if he had not been imprisoned in the camp.[41]

Both of these cases appear to involve harm. But both are stipulated to be cases where the person is better off as a result of the harm.

In light of such cases (and other problem cases), Harman gives the following sufficient condition for harm (she gives no necessary condition): 'An action harms a person if the action causes pain, early death, bodily damage, or deformity to her, even if she would not have existed had the action not been performed.'[42] Both the rape victim and the Nazi prisoner suffer harms according to Harman's condition, but not according to DMPH.

What these cases show is that it is important to distinguish between all-things-considered harms—or harms that are bad for a person taking into account all their effects on that person—and prima facie harms, or harms that are bad for a person in one way, but might also be good for that person in another more important way. DMPH is an account of all-things-considered harm, not prima facie harm. I am inclined to endorse the following account of prima facie harm: Something is a prima facie harm for a person if and only if either (i) it is intrinsically bad for that person, or (ii) it brings about something intrinsically bad for that person, or (iii) it prevents something intrinsically good for that person. Call this view **PFH**. PFH might entail Harman's sufficient condition, so long as bodily injury and deformity are intrinsically bad (which seems false, but let that pass). The rape victim and the Nazi prisoner in Harman's

---

[40] Woodward 1986, 809–11. [41] Harman 2004, 99.
[42] Harman 2004, 107.

examples both suffer prima facie harm according to PFH. But neither is the victim of an all-things-considered harm according to DMPH.[43]

The fact that neither the rape victim nor the Nazi prisoner is the victim of an all-things-considered harm does not entail that those who perpetrated prima facie harms against them did nothing wrong, nor that they do not deserve punishment for their actions. Surely the rapist and the Nazi failed to maximize expected utility by doing what they did. Both *attempted* to commit all-things-considered harms.[44] They also committed prima facie harms without the consent, and against the will, of the subjects. Certainly they violated the rights of the victims. Any of these facts could be grounds for saying that wrong actions were committed. It is surely false to say that an act is wrong only if it causes an all-things-considered harm. (Even a consequentialist can say this, as I show in Chapter 4.) This is not to say that all prima facie harmful acts are grounds for punishment. Surgeons regularly perform actions that are prima facie harmful, but in typical cases, the surgeon maximizes expected utility, acts with the consent of the patient, and violates no rights.

Being careful about the difference between prima facie and all-things-considered harms can help account for some apparently difficult cases. But there are some cases for which it will be no help. Suppose Max murders his elderly, dying uncle in order to get his inheritance. Suppose, also, that the murder is done in a way that inflicts no pain; that Max's uncle in fact had no more of a good life to look forward to, but instead would have experienced a significant amount of pain before dying; that Max's uncle desired to stay alive despite all these facts; and that the satisfaction of this desire would not have benefited Max's uncle. We might wish to describe Max's murderous action as harmful to his uncle; after all, he killed him against his will. But Max's action seems not to qualify as even a prima facie harm, given the stipulations of the example. He does

---

[43] In a footnote, Harman makes it clear that she is not talking about all-things-considered harm (Harman 2004, 109 n. 12). So her sufficient condition should be interpreted as a condition for prima facie harm, and therefore compatible with DMPH. Harman maintains that harms that are not all-things-considered harms may still function as reasons; I take no stand on this issue.

[44] For much more along these lines, see Norcross 2005, 150–1.

not cause anything intrinsically bad to happen to his uncle, since the killing is painless; he does not prevent anything intrinsically good from happening to him, given his bleak future; and, we may suppose, the killing itself is not *intrinsically* bad for the uncle. So there is no prima facie harm according to PFH; a fortiori, there is no all-things-considered harm either. So it seems neither DMPH nor PFH entail that there is a harm here.

But is this really the wrong result? I do not think so. This case illustrates a sort of *moralistic fallacy* we sometimes commit when thinking about harm.[45] Max's bad intentions and evil character lead us to think of his act as harmful; we find it hard to withhold any terms of disapprobation from his act. But imagine that Max's uncle had died in a very similar way, only without being murdered. For example, suppose that, instead of his heart failing as a result of Max giving him a lethal injection, his heart had failed due to natural causes. Suppose all the other features of the example are the same—in particular, suppose Max's uncle had nothing good to look forward to at all, and would have suffered a while longer had his heart not failed. Would his heart failure constitute a harm to him? I do not see how it could. His heart failure seems clearly beneficial to him. So what reason could there be to call Max's action harmful? Its effects on Max's uncle are exactly the same. The obvious explanation is that we are led to call his act harmful because of his bad intentions and his evil character. This is just a mistake.[46] Although his character might be relevant to whether or not he is blameworthy, and his intentions might be relevant to whether or not he should be incarcerated, neither can be relevant to whether his act is harmful. To think intentions and character could be relevant to harmfulness would be to deny the following plausible principle: if two events have *exactly the same consequences* for people, then one is harmful if and only if the other is.

Suppose I'm wrong about this; suppose that events that have the same consequences for people can be differently harmful depending on facts about intentions. This would not show that *death* from non-intentional causes is any less harmful than we previously thought.

[45] See D'Arms and Jacobson (2000) for discussion of a similar moralistic fallacy.
[46] For a similar argument see Norcross 2005, 151.

What it would show is that there are ways for other events—namely, actions—to be harmful to people apart from their consequences. An event can be harmful in the consequentialist way described by DMPH, but if it is an action, it can also be harmful in some non-consequentialist way having to do with the intentions of the person doing it. If that is so, then DMPH should be taken as a view about consequentialist harm, rather than about harm full stop. Since my concern is with the badness and harmfulness of death (rather than the harmfulness of *acts* that *cause* deaths), and the harmfulness of *death itself* is exhausted by the consequentialist account of harm, I can for the purposes of this book safely ignore the possibility of non-consequentialist harm.

2.5 An Argument For the Difference-Making Principle

So far I have noted two basic strategies for attacking DMP (or DMPH). One is to show that there are events that are bad according to DMP but are not 'genuine' evils, or are not harmful, such as not finding Aladdin's lamp. Another is to show that there are events that are genuinely bad or harmful but are not bad or harmful according to DMP or DMPH, such as the Young Pedestrian's death (and overdetermination and preemption cases more generally) and the acts performed in the examples given by Woodward and Harman. I've tried to show that these cases are not so problematic for DMP and DMPH after all. I will now argue that, for whatever alternative account of badness (or harm) someone might suggest, DMP (or DMPH) defeats that account in a head-to-head matchup.

The argument goes like this. Suppose someone proposes an account of the values of events for people. Call the account M. Suppose M is incompatible with DMP, so that some things are bad for people according to DMP (DMP-bad) but not according to M, and some things are bad for people according to M (M-bad) but not according to DMP. Now suppose someone is in the position of deciding whether to suffer an M-bad or DMP-bad event. It seems clear that, insofar as she cares about her welfare, she should choose the M-bad event.

An example will make this clearer. Recall the example of the Young Pedestrian. We might take this example to show that CPV (the causal view) should be preferred over DMP, since CPV seems to entail that the Young Pedestrian's death is very bad, but if we hold the past fixed so that the Young Pedestrian would have died from the aneurysm even if he had avoided the bus, DMP entails that his death was not very bad for him. The Young Pedestrian's actual death causes many good things not to happen to him, making his death very bad for him according to CPV; but most of those things would not have happened even if his actual death had not occurred, making his death not very bad according to DMP. But does this really provide support for CPV over DMP? Suppose the Young Pedestrian has complete knowledge of what would happen were the bus not to hit him. It would seem that he would have not much reason at all to care whether the bus hits him, insofar as he is concerned about his own welfare. If CPV is incompatible with DMP, then CPV presupposes that causes are not difference-makers; but *it is the difference-makers that we care about.* Certainly the Young Pedestrian's reasons for caring whether the bus hits him are far weaker than they would be if he had another fifty years of life to look forward to. (Of course, he might care about some more complicated event consisting of the bus hitting him and his having an aneurysm, since the combination of the bus and the aneurysm does make a big difference to how well his life goes.) So it is the DMP-badness that he should care about, not the CPV-badness.

I would give an exactly analogous argument in support of DMPH as an account of all-things-considered harm. Furthermore, for the reasons just stated, if someone were to provide a convincing argument that some other account of harm does better than DMPH at accounting for our ordinary concept of all-things-considered harm, I would say that we have a principled reason to think that our ordinary concept of harm is not of great importance. The reason, once again, is that *what matters are the difference-makers.* I care more about not being worse off than I do about not being harmed. Faced with the choice between something that harms me but leaves me no worse off, and something that leaves me worse off without harming me, I prefer the harm; to prefer otherwise would be irrational. If a harm is not a difference-maker, it merits no worrying.

To see how DMPH defeats another view, consider David Suits's view about harm. Suits makes a tripartite distinction among (alleged) harms. There are *intrinsic* harms, such as pains; *derivative* harms, such as events that cause pains; and *relational* harms, such as not winning the lottery (where no pain is involved).[47] According to Suits, relational harms are not harms at all, unless they are also intrinsic or derivative harms. If an event merely deprives me of some goods, but I get no pain as a result, and could never possibly find out about the deprivation, then I have not been harmed at all.[48] In short: an event is a harm to a person only if it is, or could be, intrinsically or derivatively harmful to that person. Call such events *Suits-harms*. Now suppose that unbeknownst to me, Ned has left me tickets to a baseball game, and Hud has subsequently stolen them from my mailbox. I would have been much happier going to the game than staying at home, but I never find out about the tickets (and, let us say, I never could find out either). Hud's theft is a DMPH-harm to me, but not a Suits-harm. Surely, a bystander who cared about my well-being would discourage Hud from stealing the tickets! If so, it is DMPH-harmfulness that matters to well-being, not Suits-harmfulness.

This may be even clearer in the case of benefits. Suppose a vaccination prevents me from experiencing great pain, and causes nothing good to happen to me. A difference-making view of benefits would entail, correctly, that the vaccination is beneficial for me. Surely it would be irrational for me not to care whether I receive the vaccination. But it is purely a *relational* benefit; it is not intrinsically good, nor is it derivatively good (in Suits's sense). So it would seem that Suits's view entails that the vaccination fails to benefit me (or that benefits and harms are not to be treated symmetrically—but why?).

Those who would like the concept of all-things-considered harm to remain a concept of significance should endorse DMPH. And if

[47] Suits 2004, 266–7.
[48] Suits 2004, 272. See Fischer 2006 for critical discussion of Suits's claim that it matters that it is possible to find out about a deprivation, even if you actually do not find out.

death makes us comparatively worse off without harming us, as Suits believes, the fact that death does not harm us should give us no comfort at all.

This does not conclude the defense of DMP. Much of the rest of this book will be devoted to attempting to solve puzzles that arise for someone who accepts DMP, to defending DMP against various arguments designed to show that DMP does not provide an adequate account of the value of death, and to presenting arguments against DMP's competitors.

3

EXISTENCE AND TIME

So death, the most terrifying of ills, is nothing to us, since so long as we exist, death is not with us; but when death comes, then we do not exist. It does not then concern either the living or the dead, since for the former it is not, and the latter are no more.

Epicurus, 'Letter to Menoeceus'

EPICURUS might be interpreted as endorsing the following premises: (1) Anything that is bad for someone must be bad for that person at a particular time. (2) There is no time at which death is bad for the one who dies. (Death is not bad for someone before she dies, since it has not occurred yet; it is not bad for her once she dies, because from that point on *she* no longer exists.) Therefore, (3) death is not bad for the one who dies. Whether this is Epicurus' argument or not, it is worth considering, since, if sound, it undermines the difference-making principle (DMP). What's more, some find the argument persuasive,[1] and even among those who find the argument unsound, there is no consensus about where it goes wrong.

While I am not entirely convinced that (1) is true, I think there is more reason to accept (1) than to accept (2), though (1) is far more commonly rejected. So my main goals here will be to show that there is some cost associated with rejecting (1), to argue that there are good reasons to reject (2), and to provide a positive account of the time at

---

[1] See Marquis 1985, 160; Nussbaum 1994, 201–2; Mothersill 1999, 20; Rosenbaum 1993; and Suits 2004.

which death is bad for the one who dies. Roughly, I will argue that death is bad for the person who dies at all and only those times when the person would have been living well, or living a life worth living, had she not died when she did.[2]

3.1 Is All Badness Temporal?

Recall the first premise of the argument:

> *Premise 1: Anything that is bad for someone must be bad for that person at a particular time.*

Epicurus never explicitly states this premise—it is just required to make his argument valid—and he says nothing to defend it. So why should we accept it? Consider an ordinary case of badness. In the summer of 2006 I badly stubbed my left pinky toe while walking in the dark. It hurt a lot for a little while. It hurt a fair bit for several days afterwards. After about a week, it pretty much stopped hurting. At what times was the toe-stubbing bad for me? This question seems to have an obvious answer. It was worst for me for a little while after it happened. It was bad for me, but somewhat less bad, for the ensuing week. It is not bad for me now at all. The duration of the harm is limited and, in principle, easily locatable.

This is just one example of a bad thing that is bad for me at a particular time. It can hardly show that Premise 1 is true. But when we think about *why* the toe-stubbing is bad, we might be led to believe Premise 1. The toe-stubbing is bad *because of* what happens at those times after the toe-stubbing. If not for the fact that it caused me to

---

[2] This is only a chit-chatty statement of my view; see Section 3.4. The view I defend is similar to one suggested by William Grey: 'The temporal location of the harm of Ramsey's untimely death, I suggest, is the time when Ramsey might have lived' (Grey 1999, 364). John Fischer says something that seems very similar: 'The subject of the misfortune is you (the individual who dies). The time of the misfortune is the time during which you are dead' (Fischer 1997, 352). However, Fischer's reasons for saying so are different from mine. Fischer endorses this view because he thinks it is intrinsically bad to be betrayed, and betrayals may occur posthumously.

suffer harm at those later times, the toe-stubbing would not have been bad. This suggests that it is essential, at least to a certain sort of harm, that it be bad at a particular time.

Of course, there could be other sorts of harm that are timeless. But if it turned out that death were the only such harm, we might have reason to be suspicious. Why should death be unique among evils? Are there other examples of timeless evils we might appeal to in order to reduce suspicions about death?

According to Thomas Nagel, while the subject of a misfortune 'can be exactly located in a sequence of places and times, the same is not necessarily true of the goods and ills that befall him.'[3] In support of this claim, Nagel describes a man who has suffered severe brain damage, reducing him to the status of a contented infant. Nagel says that Epicurus' questions about the time when death is bad for the one who dies can also be raised about this brain-damaged man and the time when the brain damage is bad for him. There is no reason to pity this man now, because he is content; the intelligent man he used to be no longer exists (or so says Nagel), so we cannot pity him either.

Nagel uses this example to support his view about death.

If we apply to death the account suggested for the case of dementia, we shall say that although the spatial and temporal locations of the individual who suffered the loss are clear enough, the misfortune itself cannot be so easily located. One must be content just to state that his life is over and there will never be any more of it. That fact, rather than his past or present condition, constitutes his misfortune, if it is one.[4]

Nagel's strategy seems to be to show that badness is atemporal in cases not involving death, and therefore there is no problem with saying that the badness of death is atemporal. But Nagel's argument

---

[3] Nagel 1979, 5.

[4] Nagel 1979, 7. Grey points out that Nagel does not explicitly say that the evil of death is timeless; he merely says it 'cannot be *so easily* located' in time (Grey 1999, 362–3). Perhaps he did not mean to say that the evil of death cannot be located *at all*, but merely that it cannot be *easily* or *precisely* located. If that is Nagel's view, I do not disagree with it so far as it goes; but it does not go far enough to answer the question at hand.

is unconvincing. First of all, it is not clear that the contented infant example can provide any independent support for the atemporality of the badness of death. In the example, the person who existed before the accident is stipulated not to exist anymore. Perhaps this makes it a case of death (where the person who dies is replaced by another person with diminished mental capacities); or perhaps it makes it a case where a person goes out of existence without (or before) dying. Either way, the very same metaphysical problems arise in this sort of case as in a case of death. So nothing can be gained by the analogy.[5] The Epicurean will say the very same thing about the contented infant case that he says about death: namely, that you cannot be harmed by going out of existence and being replaced by a contented infant. And if the person is not stipulated to go out of existence at the time of the brain damage, then the timing problem goes away. The person who is to be pitied is the person sitting here, as content as an infant. Perhaps it is only by looking at the person's past that we can recognize this as a misfortune for him; nevertheless, it is his present condition that constitutes his misfortune, if it is one.

Here is a somewhat complicated example of an apparently timeless evil. Suppose that Andy is trying to decide whether to get married, and decides to flip a coin. If it lands heads, he'll get married, otherwise not. Just before he can flip the coin he sustains a head injury at time t4 (see Figure 3.1), resulting in Andy's living out the remaining twenty years of his life with no good or bad experiences. He is still conscious and alive, but destined to have a mediocre life. Now suppose that if Andy had flipped the coin and it came up heads, he would have experienced ten years of extreme happiness after t4, followed by ten years of moderate unhappiness. Call this life L1. If it had come up tails, he would have experienced ten years of moderate unhappiness after t4, followed by ten years of extreme happiness. Call this life L2. In both L1 and L2, the degree of unhappiness felt during the unhappy period would have been severe enough that a life consisting *merely* of experiences like that would not be worth living, and that Andy would slightly prefer being comatose to having those experiences;

---

[5] Martha Nussbaum (1994, 205–6), and Frederik Kaufman (2004, 243) make similar points about Nagel's example.

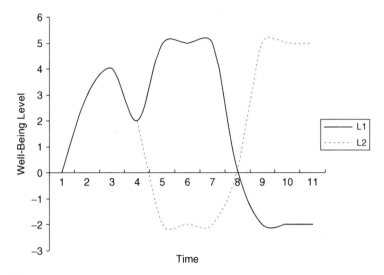

Figure 3.1

but the degree of happiness felt during the extremely happy period would have far outweighed the unhappiness contained in the unhappy period. Finally, suppose that there is no fact of the matter concerning whether the coin would have come up heads or tails had he flipped it—perhaps because there is no fact of the matter concerning exactly *how* he would have flipped the coin if he had flipped it.[6] It would seem that given these assumptions, there is no time such that we can say that Andy's injury is bad for him at that time. At any given time, there are two ways his life could have been going, one good and one bad. One life is better for Andy than his actual life at that time, and one life is worse. Intuitively, Andy's injury was bad for him. Both L1 and L2 are overall worthwhile existences; hence, Andy's injury at t deprived him of an existence that would have been much better on the whole than his actual comatose existence.

There might be other examples of timeless evils. Perhaps the evil of never seeing one's beloved again is an example of a timeless evil;

---

[6] Note that there is no need to presuppose indeterminism here.

never getting what one deserves might be another such example.[7] So should we just admit that there are timeless evils, and say that death is one such evil? I think this would be rash. It is important to remember why death is supposed to be bad for us. Death prevents us from doing things we want to do, and experiencing things we want to experience. In this way it is like sicknesses and injuries, except that the latter are not permanent, and typically cause us pain in addition to preventing us from doing things. If this is so, it seems preferable to have an account of the evil of death that makes its evilness similar to that of the evils of ordinary sicknesses and injuries.[8] Rejecting Epicurus' argument by claiming that death is a timeless evil should be regarded as a fallback position.

More cautiously: It might be that death is bad for us in various ways. Perhaps part of its badness is timeless. It might cause its victim never to get what he deserves, and never to see his beloved again. If such evils are timeless, then perhaps part of death's badness is timeless. But philosophers have been too quick to claim that death is a timeless evil, or that questions about the timing of its badness are misguided, on the basis of these sorts of examples.[9] Even if death is bad in these ways, *it also seems bad in other ways*, similar to the ways in which sickness and injury are bad. Sickness and injury are timeful evils. So it is best to have a theory that entails that *at least part* of the evil of death is timeful.[10] Otherwise we open the door for a more moderate Epicurean to argue that death, while indeed bad, is not nearly as bad as we thought; it is not as bad as other evils that harm us in both timeless and timeful ways.

In Section 3.3 I will show how to treat some apparently timeless evils as timeful evils. But first, we must examine Premise 2.

---

[7] I thank an anonymous referee for these examples.

[8] This argument is similar to one given by Feit (2002, 361). Christopher Williams claims that 'the deprivation theorist typically insists that death has a nearly *sui generis* character: that missing out on life is not like missing out on something in life' (Williams 2007, 271). He does not provide any examples of such theorists, but if he is right, then I am not like most deprivation theorists.

[9] Nagel 1979; Silverstein 1980.

[10] Julian Lamont argues that Nagel's view should be rejected in light of the fact that it entails that there are causes that have effects that obtain at no time (Lamont 1998, 208).

3.2 Could Death Be a Temporal Evil?

Recall Premise 2:

Premise 2: There is no time at which death is bad for the one who dies.

Feldman gives this evocative description of Epicurus' reasoning: 'At the very moment when the Reaper clutches us in his bony embrace, we go out of existence. Since the nonexistent cannot be harmed, death cannot harm us.'[11] But why should we need to exist while dead in order for death to harm us? We need some general principle to support this line of reasoning.

Epicurus' defense of Premise 2 seems to presuppose the truth of hedonism. Upon our deaths, we can no longer experience any pain; thus if hedonism is true, death cannot be bad for us at any time after we die, since it cannot cause us any pain. A natural move would be to reject hedonism, as Nagel does (though Nagel seems to accept Premise 2).[12] One might say that it is possible to be the subject of intrinsic evil without being able to experience anything—for example, by being the subject of a nasty rumor. But this view is unnecessarily contentious; surely there is a way to account for the evil of death without claiming that the dead can be subjects of *intrinsic* evil.[13] Recall that one of the nice features of DMP is that it is flexible: it assumes no substantive theory of well-being. It would be better not to give up that nice feature if it is not necessary to do so. Furthermore, as we've seen in Chapter 1, correspondence theories of well-being face serious problems, so it would be best if a reply to Epicurus did not require us to endorse such a theory. We should be able to respond to Epicurus from within a hedonistic framework. So let us suppose, for now, that pure hedonism is true.

Hedonism, by itself, cannot establish Premise 2. Epicurus saw a problem in attributing disvalue to death only because he assumed that the only things that can be good or bad for a person are sensations;

---

[11] Feldman 1992, 4.   [12] Nagel 1979.
[13] Walter Glannon claims that Nagel's view is that such evils are merely extrinsically bad (Glannon 2001, 132). But this cannot be right, for it leaves us with no explanation for Nagel's rejection of hedonism.

since nonexistent people do not have sensations, nothing good or bad can happen to them. But while it is at least arguable, and hedonists assert, that the only things that can be *intrinsically* good or bad for someone are sensations, sensations are not the only things that can be *extrinsically* good or bad for someone. In particular, the *causes* and *preventors* of our sensations, anything that *makes a difference* to our experiences, may be extrinsically good or bad for us. Deprivation theorists attribute extrinsic value, not intrinsic value, to death; death causes us not to have any sensations, which is worse for us than having good sensations. Since Epicurus' defense of Premise 2 was based on the fact that there are no times while one is dead at which one is in pain, it might be thought that we can reject Premise 2 merely by noticing that death is bad for us in this other way: by preventing us from having good experiences. This does not require posthumous pain.

The move to extrinsic value undercuts one bad justification for Premise 2. But it does not answer Epicurus' real question: *at what time* is a person's death bad for her? One might wonder how anything can be even extrinsically bad for someone at a time when the person does not exist. This is what has been called the 'problem of the subject': if the dead person is not here now, how can her death be bad for her now? The basis of this worry needs to be more carefully identified.

The no-subject problem might stem from a general principle about relations: in order for a relation to relate things, it must relate them at a time, and in order for a relation to relate things at a time, both *relata* must exist at that time. For example, my computer cannot be on my desk right now unless both my computer and my desk exist right now. Therefore, the badness-for relation can hold between a state of affairs or event and a person only at times when the person exists; so nothing can be bad for a person at times when she does not exist. Thus, there is no time at which death is bad for the one who dies.

That principle about relations is too strong. Many garden-variety, non-death-related events are good or bad for a person long after the *events* are over, and thus seem to relate an existing thing to a nonexisting thing. Consider my toe-stubbing. That event went out of existence, but continued to be bad for me for a week afterwards.[14] We might then ask: how could the particular event consisting of me stubbing my toe still be bad for me at a time when that event no longer exists? The badness-for relation would be relating something that exists—me—with something that does not exist anymore—a particular toe-stubbing event that occurred earlier. Yet there is no controversy over whether toe-stubbings could really be bad for us. There seem to be many other examples of relations that hold between an existing thing and a nonexisting thing, most having nothing to do with goodness or badness. The is-a-great-great-grandson-of relation often relates an existing person and a nonexistent person. Causal relations between events somehow relate events that do not overlap in time. Semantic relations sometimes relate words, or mental events, to things that existed long ago in the past but no longer exist (like Socrates). Some relations even seem to relate things at times when neither thing exists; for example, the is-a-more-popular-former-President-than relation currently relates Abraham Lincoln and James K. Polk, neither of whom currently exists. The no-subject problem cannot be defended by appeal to any such general principle about relations.

The counterexamples to the principle about relations just discussed share an interesting feature: they are all problematic for *presentists*. Presentism is the view that only present objects exist—there are no past or future things.[15] Eternalism, on the other hand, is the view that past and future objects exist. They do not exist *now*, but they exist, much in the way that objects may exist without existing *here*. The eternalist thinks of existence-at-a-time in the same way as existence-at-a-place. These are not different sorts of existence; rather, one may bear the *located-at* relation to a place or to a time (one bears that relation, most fundamentally, to a *space–time region*). Perhaps presentism underlies the no-subject worry, in the following way. Attribution of badness to someone's death requires us to locate

---

[14] Of course, the event-*type* might continue to exist. However, I presume that if we accept an event-ontology, particular event *tokens* are often good or bad for us. (I leave open the possibility that we might also want to say that event types are good or bad for us.)

[15] See Sider 2001, II, and Markosian 2004.

an individual for whom the death is bad. If presentism is true, then
once a person dies, there is no person for whom the death could be
bad. If Premise 2 of Epicurus' argument presupposes the truth of
presentism, then rejecting presentism might help us answer Epicurus.
If the past is real, there is no difficulty in locating a subject of the
evil of death; it is a past person.[16] Rejecting presentism is a good idea
for other reasons, including the need to preserve our ability to refer
to past objects like Socrates and to account for the literal truth of
our history books. If attributions of badness to death are in the same
boat as references to Socrates, they are in good company. Rejecting
presentism, and believing in the reality of the past, seems to solve
the no-subject problem.[17] We might put things in the following way.
Epicurus thought that people could not coexist with their deaths,
because there is no time at which a person and her death coexist.
Without coexistence, death cannot be bad for its victim. But, goes
the reply, eternalism provides coexistence: a person and her death
coexist, not at a time, but in the space–time manifold.

I am not as excited about this response as I used to be.[18] Presentists
believe they are entitled to say many of the same things about death
that the eternalists can say. For example, suppose we are talking
about a living, currently existing person. Since the presentist believes
this person exists, the presentist believes there are now singular
propositions about that person—propositions that are directly about
her, or directly involve her in some way. Among those propositions
are future-tensed propositions about how things will be going for her
after she is dead. So there can now be a future-tensed proposition
to the effect that her death will harm her at some particular time in

---

[16] Kai Draper suggests a response to the Epicurean that may amount to the
same thing: 'I suspect that it makes sense to speak of the dead as occupying a level
of well-being because it is possible to refer to the living person who was, and to
assign this *past-existent* a level of well-being in the present based on the no doubt
limited extent to which he is now being benefited or harmed' (Draper 1999, 404;
his emphasis). Also see Draper 2004, 102.

[17] For an example of the sort of odd position one can be led to by endorsing
presentism and also maintaining that death is bad for its victim, see Yourgrau
1987.

[18] See Bradley 2004 for my argument, which I now believe to be unsound, that
rejecting presentism solves the no-subject problem.

the future. So there is no problem with saying that her death will be bad for her, and that it will be bad for her at times after she is dead. Whatever story presentists tell about what makes such propositions true, they can tell it about these propositions. Presentists do not face a no-subject problem concerning presently existing people.

This is not to say that presentists do not face any problems in this vicinity. For the aforementioned singular propositions go out of existence once the victim dies. *At that point*, there are no singular propositions about her anymore; a fortiori, there are no propositions about how well things are going for her, about how bad her death was for her, or attributing such badness to any particular times. Thus we can no longer meaningfully say, *of her*, that her death was bad for her. (We can perhaps say things that are closely related, e.g. that someone fitting such-and-such description was harmed by dying. But this is not to say anything directly about any person.) So there is a problem for presentists here, but it is not particularly related to the problem of locating a time at which death is bad for someone. It is just a problem about how to ground truths about past things and people.[19] The presentist must have some general story to tell about such truths; that story should just be applied to truths about dead people, e.g. that their deaths were bad for them. I doubt a sufficiently plausible story can be told; but if it can, all the better for the anti-Epicurean, since it follows that we need not be committed to any particular view about the reality of the past in order to account for the badness of death.

Since presentism offers insufficient support to Epicurus, we have not yet found a general principle to underlie Premise 2. It cannot be supported by hedonism, or by the principle that the *relata* of a relation must exist at the time the relation holds, or by presentism. (At least, if presentism is the only principle supporting Premise 2, Premise 2 is in big trouble.) Why, then, should we think that there is no time at which death is bad for the one who dies? Rather than arguing from any of these general principles, the Epicurean should put forward the following challenge: 'So you think death is bad for people at particular times. Well then, which times? When you answer that question, I'll tell you why you are wrong.' In the next sections

---

[19] Sider 2001, 35–42.

I'll give my answer, explain what's wrong with alternative answers, and defend my answer against Epicurean attacks.

3.3 When Is Death Bad?

Suppose we want to say that death can be bad for someone at a particular time. We must then answer the question: *at which time?* If no satisfactory answer to this question can be given—i.e., if the answer is 'never'—then we must admit the truth of Premise 2 after all, and fall back on the timeless evil solution.

There are four possible answers to this question.[20]

Priorism: Death is bad for its victim *before* the victim dies.

Concurrentism: Death is bad for its victim *at the time* of the victim's death.

Subsequentism: Death is bad for its victim *after* the victim dies.

Eternalism: Death is *eternally* bad for its victim.[21]

Let us begin with eternalism, which is endorsed by Feldman.[22] According to DMP, when we say that S's death is bad for S, we are comparing the values for S of two possible worlds. According to Feldman, those two worlds stand in their value-relations at all times. Suppose the actual world has a value for S of +100, while the nearest world at which S's actual death does not occur has a value for S of +120. The question 'When is S's death bad for S?' then boils down to the question 'When is 120 greater than 100?' The answer, obviously, is 'always.' Therefore, Feldman says, S's death at t is bad for S eternally.[23]

---

[20] Some of this terminology is borrowed from Luper 2006, and Luper 2007, 241. I ignore a fifth option, *indefinitism*, since it is compatible with at least some of the four views stated here.

[21] Note that this is, obviously, a different view from the just-discussed *ontological* eternalism.

[22] Feldman 1991, 221.

[23] Feldman has since clarified his view (personal correspondence). Feldman's current view is that death is bad for the one who dies, not at all specific times

I think Feldman's view does express something true—or at least, it correctly answers one possible question we might be considering—but as Julian Lamont correctly points out, it leaves the interesting question unanswered.[24] Even if determining the badness of a death for a person involves a comparison of possible worlds, it still seems wrong to say that if a world is good for a person, it is good for that person at all times; a person's death does not remain bad for him thousands of years after it occurs, nor was it bad for him before he died, or before he even existed. To say such things is no more plausible than saying that my toe-stubbing harmed me even before it happened.

The problem is that there are at least two different things we might be asking when we ask when someone's death is bad for that person. Neil Feit clearly describes this difference:

Consider again the question: When is Abe Lincoln's death bad for him? Feldman takes the question to be equivalent to this: When is it true that his death is bad for him? Hence Feldman is led to his version of eternalism about the evil of death. On the other hand, I take the question to be asking this: At which times t is it true that his death is bad for him at t?[25]

We may understand this second question to be asking a question about the 'badness-at-a-time-for' relation: At which times t is it true that S's death is bad-at-t for S? In other words: given that death makes its victim worse off, which are the times such that the death makes its victim worse off at those times than she would have been at those times if the death had not occurred? Eternalism does not give us a plausible answer to this question. There is no death that makes its victim worse off, at times before she was born, than she would have been if the death had not occurred.

within a world (as seems to be his view in his 1991), but *from the perspective of eternity*—a point of view that stands outside all possible worlds. Thus Feldman can deny that someone's death is bad at a specific time within a world before that person exists. This makes his view more plausible, but makes it essentially similar to Nagel's view. I reject Feldman's clarified view for the same reason I reject Nagel's: namely, I think we may also want to say that death can be bad for its victim at particular times within a world.

[24] Lamont 2002, 199.

[25] Feit 2002, 372–3. Julian Lamont and Harry Silverstein give similar criticisms of Feldman's view (Lamont 1998, 199–200; Silverstein 2000, 120–1).

We might reject concurrentism for a similar reason: that it is motivated by a misconstrual of the question. The question is not: When does the instrumentally bad event occur? The question is: When is the instrumentally bad event bad for its victim? When it comes to other bad events, we do not think the time of the badness is the time of the instrumentally bad event. If tomorrow I drink a vial of poison that results in my having a torturous sickness next week, the drinking is not bad for me tomorrow, but next week.

Concurrentism need not be motivated by such a misconstrual. Steven Luper claims that in addition to being an evil of deprivation, death is also an evil of destruction. Death destroys important human capacities. That destruction rarely takes place in an instant; it occurs over a period of time. The time of the badness of that destruction, says Luper, is when the destruction takes place. 'The subject of death is a live creature; death harms (at least in part) by destroying that creature's vital capacities; and that harm occurs at the very time the creature dies.'[26] But whether the destruction of capacities occurs in an instant or over a period of time, it seems wrong to say that all of its badness is contained in the time of its occurrence. We can see this by reflecting on why this destruction is bad. Consider two people whose important capacities are *temporarily* destroyed in identical ways—that is, the process of destruction is identical. For one, the capacities return after five minutes. For the other, they return after a year plus five minutes. Thus, the second deprives its victim of an extra year of the exercise of those capacities. Which destruction was worse? Clearly it is the second. What this shows is that the destruction of capacities is itself, at least in large part, an evil of deprivation. In this case, it would seem that the time of the badness of the destruction of capacities is the time when one lives without those capacities—but the important thing to note is that the time of the badness is not, at least primarily, the time of the destruction.

Perhaps it is also *intrinsically* bad to have one's capacities destroyed. This seems questionable to me, and Luper never explicitly makes any such claim. But even if it is true, the example of the previous paragraph shows that this is not the only way in which this destruction

[26] Luper 2006.

is bad. If having one's capacities destroyed is bad, this badness must be only a small part of the badness. We still need to locate a time, other than the time of the destruction itself, when the destruction is bad.

Next consider priorism. Philosophers are led to priorism in the following way. What is bad about death is that it frustrates our interests or desires. Those interests or desires exist only while we are alive. So death retroactively makes our lives worse by making it the case that the desires or interests we have while alive are frustrated. This view is very popular; it has been held by Joel Feinberg and George Pitcher, among many others.[27]

Priorism is problematic. First, priorism seems either to yield counterintuitive results about non-death-related harms, or to entail that the evil of death is very different from other evils. As pointed out in Section 1.3, if yesterday I desired that it not snow today, but it is snowing today, things were not going badly for me *yesterday*. If anything, they are going badly *today*. Priorism requires that we either give up this judgment about snow, or say that death is different. If we say that death is different, we should wonder why it is different; and this explanation invariably involves the supposition that the other possible ways to account for the time of death's badness (especially subsequentism) are unacceptable. So we can undercut the motivation for priorism by establishing that subsequentism is a coherent position.

Another strike against priorism is that, at least in its most popular incarnations, it presupposes a correspondence theory of welfare.[28] The fact that the view presupposes any theory of welfare at all makes it less attractive. It's better to solve Epicurus' timing problem without having to take a stand on another issue that is, if anything, larger, more complicated, and more controversial. And as we've seen in Chapter 1, correspondence theories bring along serious problems. Again, if the *only* way to locate the badness of death in time were

[27] See, for example, Feinberg 1993; Pitcher 1993; Li 1999; Luper 2004; Luper 2007; and Bigelow, Campbell, and Pargetter 1990.

[28] Non-correspondence theories, such as narrative structure theories, might also be compatible with priorism. But priorists typically think death is bad for its victim in virtue of its frustrating the victim's desires, interrupting her projects, etc., and that it is bad at the time the desire is held, or the efforts are made. Thus they are correspondence theorists.

to accept priorism and some appropriate theory of well-being, it might be reasonable to overlook those problems for correspondence theories; but since priorism seems motivated mostly by the view that subsequentism is metaphysically untenable, we must determine whether this is so.

Subsequentism is the view that death is bad for its victim after the victim has died. Subsequentism seems clearly correct as an account of when ordinary events are good or bad for people.[29] Return to my toe-stubbing case; let t_1 be the time I stubbed my toe. Let us say the discomfort lasts seven days, and prevents me from hiking or playing tennis during that time, which I would have enjoyed doing. Suppose the toe-stubbing does not have any lingering effects. It does not prevent me from completing this book, does not cause me to lose my job, and is soon forgotten. Intuitively, we should say that my stubbing my toe at t_1 is (extrinsically) bad for me during my seven days of discomfort after t_1, but once I recover it is no longer bad for me.[30]

It seems to me that the reason we say that my stubbing my toe at t_1 is bad for me during the seven days following t_1 is that my life would have been going better for me during that time had I not stubbed my toe. That is, the intrinsic value of the portion of my life that takes place during the seven days after t_1 is lower than it would have been had I not stubbed my toe. It also seems that my stubbing my toe is no longer bad for me once the pain goes away and I am able to resume my normal activities. Its effect on me, and on the value of my life, is over.

In light of the plausibility of subsequentism about toe-stubbings, it is odd that subsequentism is sometimes not even mentioned as a possible view one might have about the time of death's badness.[31] For

---

[29] Luper concedes this point but thinks subsequentism is unacceptable anyway; see Luper 2007, 242.

[30] I assume that injuries and sicknesses are merely extrinsically bad for people, in virtue of the fact that they cause people pain and—at least temporarily—prevent them from doing the things they would otherwise like to be doing. Naturally, the analogy with death holds only insofar as death prevents people from doing and experiencing things, since being dead does not cause pain to the one who dies.

[31] For example, Julian Lamont and Jack Li omit subsequentism from their lists of possible answers to the timing problem (Lamont 1998; Li 1999).

it is not hard to see how to say something basically similar in the case of death. The death of S at t_1 is bad for S at t_2, where t_2 is later than t_1, provided that at t_2, the life S would have been living had S not died at t_1 would have been better for S than no life at all. Thus, Socrates' death has long ceased to be bad for Socrates, since had he not died when he did, he would still have been dead for many years; but Anna Nicole Smith's death might still be bad for her today, since she might well be living happily had she not died when she did. Of course, there is one difference that might prove to be important that should be flagged immediately: in the case of death, the victim (arguably) ceases to exist. We will return to this worry later in the chapter.

In order to formulate my version of subsequentism, I need to introduce the idea of the value of a time for a person. The time when I felt pain from the toe-stubbing was a bad time for me; some of the times when Socrates was dead, but would have been alive had he not drunk the hemlock, were bad times for Socrates. As noted in Section 1.3, talk of times being good or bad for people is ubiquitous; some nostalgic types say that their college years were the best years of their lives; we often talk of someone who is going through a bad time right now. Determining the values of times for people is crucial to answering questions about the time of the evil of death.

How do we determine the value of a time for a person? In Section 1.2.1, we introduced the notion of the intrinsic value of a *world* for a person. I think that the intrinsic value of a *time* for a person ought to be determined in a similar way. On a simple view, to determine the intrinsic value of a world for a person, we add up the intrinsic values of the value atoms that are (i) about that person and (ii) part of that world. We might determine the intrinsic value of a time for a person as follows:

IVT. The intrinsic value of a time for a person = the sum, for all value atoms obtaining at that time, of their values for that person.

Some features of IVT are worth pointing out, as they will become relevant later. First, IVT is just a more specific version of internalism (see Section 1.3), since it entails that how well things go for a person at a time is entirely determined by the intrinsic values of states obtaining at that time. The intrinsic values of states obtaining at other times are irrelevant. IVT does not, however, presuppose the stronger principle I defended in Section 1.3: SUP, or the principle that the intrinsic value of a state of affairs is determined independently of the values of any other states. While I think SUP is justified, and the arguments of Section 1.3 support SUP, defending SUP is not necessary for my purposes in this chapter. IVT is compatible with views about intrinsic value according to which the intrinsic value of something can depend on its relations to other things.

Second, IVT allows us to determine how well things go for someone not only at instants of time, such as precisely 12 noon on Jan. 26, 2001, but also durations of time, such as the period from 12 noon to 1pm on Jan. 26, 2001. To determine the intrinsic value of a duration of time for a person, we simply look at the basic intrinsic values of all the states obtaining during that time.

We may now determine the overall value of an event for a person at a time by comparing the intrinsic value of the time for the person with what the intrinsic value of the time *would have been* for the person had that event not occurred. As in Section 2.1, we may take this to involve comparing the intrinsic value of the time for the person in the actual world with the intrinsic value of the time for the person in the nearest possible world at which the event does not occur. We may state this view, the ***Difference-Making Principle for Times***, in the following way:

> **DMPT**. The overall value of event E for subject S at world w and time t = the intrinsic value of t for S at w minus the intrinsic value of t for S at the nearest world to w at which E does not occur.[32]

In the case of death, we may assume for now that all times after a person's death have intrinsic values of zero for that person (I will return to this assumption below). DMPT inherits the internalism of IVT; it entails that the value of any event for a person at a time is wholly determined by how things go for that person at that time, in actual and counterfactual circumstances. To see how DMPT works, see Figure 3.2.

---

[32] For ease of exposition I have suppressed the relativization to similarity relations (Section 2.1).

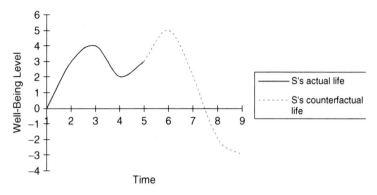

Figure 3.2

The solid line in Figure 3.2 represents the value over time of S's actual life, supposing S dies at t_5. The dotted line represents what the value of S's life would have been had S's death at t_5 not occurred. According to DMPT, S's death at t_5 is *bad* for S at times t_6 and t_7 (and for many extended periods immediately after S's death), since the intrinsic values of those times for S, at the nearest world in which S does not die at t_5, is *greater* than zero; S's death at t_5 is *good* for S at t_8 and t_9, since the intrinsic value of those times for S, at the nearest world in which S does not die at t_5, is *less* than zero.

DMPT has some nice features. First, it enables us to avoid the apparent counterexample to Premise 1 of the Epicurean argument presented in Section 3.1. In the counterexample I presented, it seemed that there was no time at which Andy's injury was bad for him. But this is true only if we are talking about moments; there are many durations at which Andy's injury can be said to be bad for him, including the twenty-year period after his death. No matter whether L_1 or L_2 would have been Andy's life, that twenty-year period would have been better for him than a life spent comatose. We might use a similar strategy to account for other apparent cases of timeless evils, such as never seeing one's beloved again or never getting what one deserves. Take the latter case; suppose Fred deserves a teaching award but never gets it. The closest possible world in which Fred gets the teaching award might be a world in which he gets the award in 2002, or it might be a world in which he gets the award in 2003. Suppose getting the award would make Fred's life better for some period of time afterwards. Then his never getting the award could be said to be bad for him during a period of time starting sometime in 2002, and ending sometime after 2003. This does not seem implausible. There might be no way, even in principle, to determine a *smaller* period of time during which his never getting the award is bad for him; but that is not enough to show that it is a timeless evil. Other apparently timeless evils could get the same treatment.[33]

Second, while I have introduced DMPT as a version of subsequentism, and it goes best with a subsequentist view, it is really a more general principle that is compatible with other views, including priorism. For example, if DMPT is combined with an attitudinalist desire satisfactionist view of well-being (Section 1.3), it entails that death may be bad for its victim before she dies—specifically, at those times before death at which she has desires that are frustrated by her death. DMPT does not commit us to such views, however. So like DMP, DMPT has an attractive flexibility.[34]

3.4 Objections

Consider the following sentence:

The Aunt Alice sentence. Aunt Alice's death was good for her during the week after she died, but bad for her during the next month.

If Aunt Alice would have been miserable for a week, then happy for a month had she not died when she did, DMPT entails that

---

[33] Grey employs this strategy for dealing with such evils: 'To say that there is no precise or *locatable* time at which harms occur is not to say there is no time at which they occur' (Grey 1999, 364; his emphasis).

[34] DMPT is not the only version of subsequentism; see Feit 2002 for another version, and see Bradley 2004 for my discussion of Feit's view.

the Aunt Alice sentence is true. Some would consider this to be a counterexample to DMPT.[35]

While the Aunt Alice sentence might sound odd, I believe sentences of the sort are often true. Let us add some detail to the story of Aunt Alice. Suppose she was suffering from a very painful illness; she underwent a risky procedure that, if successful, would have had her feeling well in a week; instead the procedure failed, and she died. Shortly after her death, we might say things like 'Aunt Alice was in so much pain; it's good that she is no longer suffering.' Later on, we might say something like 'it's too bad Aunt Alice is no longer with us; she would have enjoyed seeing little Timmy's recital.' The Aunt Alice sentence is really nothing more than a way of summing up both of these sentiments; understood in this way, the Aunt Alice sentence loses its oddness and seems true to me. Thus I do not consider the Aunt Alice sentence to be a counterexample.

Harry Silverstein gives another purported counterexample to DMPT:

[M]y mother died, at age 86, in June of 2000; and her death was at least an indirect result of, though it did not immediately follow, a serious auto accident she had the preceding winter. If, then, we compare her actual life-whole to the life-whole which would have obtained if she had not had the accident—which would seem to be an appropriate alternative life-whole to choose for the comparison; and if we consider the likely duration of that alternative, given (among other things) the history of female longevity in my family; then it would seem plausible to say that that alternative life-whole would have extended five years longer to, say, June of 2005. Well, if that is so, then on Bradley's view it would seem to have been appropriate for my sisters and me to plan a family party for some time in, say, July 2005, to celebrate the fact that, though our mother's death *had* been an evil for her through the preceding five years, it now no longer was.[36]

This criticism is misplaced. DMPT says nothing about under what circumstances, or at what times, it is appropriate to feel happy, or to

---

[35] Elizabeth Harman gave the Aunt Alice example in her comments on Bradley 2004, at the 2001 Bellingham Summer Philosophy Conference.

[36] Silverstein (forthcoming), 9. (Page references are to the manuscript version.)

throw a party. It is true that in *some* cases it seems appropriate to
have a positive reaction when an extrinsically bad event has ceased
to be bad (even if the reaction falls short of throwing a party). But
not in all cases. To see the difference, compare two examples. First,
consider the toe-stubbing example. Suppose my toe hurts for a while,
and prevents me from playing tennis. When it stops hurting, and
I can play tennis again, a positive reaction (if not a party) seems
appropriate. Second, remember the case of Hud and the stolen
baseball tickets (Section 2.5): Hud steals the tickets from my mailbox,
and as a result I am less happy during the baseball game than I
would have been if he had not stolen the tickets. When the game is
over, no positive reaction seems appropriate, even though the theft
is no longer making a difference to how things go for me. What's
the difference between these cases? In the toe-stubbing case, when
the toe-stubbing stops being bad for me, my prospects improve in
two ways. First, I am no longer in pain; there is an intrinsically bad
consequence of the toe-stubbing that ends. Second, I can now do
things I had been prevented from doing, like play tennis. Either of
these facts might warrant celebration of some sort. In the case of the
stolen baseball tickets, my prospects do not improve in either of these
ways when the theft ceases to be bad. The harm of death is more
like the harm of the stolen baseball tickets. When its harm ends, the
victim's prospects do not improve. No intrinsically bad event ends at
that time, nor does the victim regain the prospect of receiving goods
of which she had been deprived. This explains why it would have
been weird for Silverstein to throw a party.

   Silverstein offers another example he thinks is problematic for
DMPT:

[S]uppose that Ann was a writer who wrote several novels which were both
critically acclaimed and extremely popular—novels of such stature that she
could have expected to be admired for centuries after her death, in the way
that, e.g., Jane Austen has been—but that, some time after her death, her
country is taken over by a brutally repressive regime whose leaders hate her
books and manage to purge them from the culture so thoroughly that sub-
sequent generations have no knowledge whatever of her or her work. In my
view, insofar as it is reasonable to view this unfortunate purge as evil *for Ann*
at all, it is just as reasonable to view it as evil for her if it occurs, say, fifty years

after she dies (at a time when there is no appropriate alternative life-whole on which she would still be alive) as it is if it occurs ten years after she dies (at a time when she would still be alive on an appropriate alternative life-whole). But on Bradley's view, it would seem, we would have to say that the purge is an evil for her if it occurs at the earlier time, but not if it occurs at the later time.[37]

Silverstein's worry is understandable. I have sometimes stated my view, incautiously, as the view that death is bad for its victim at all the times when the person would have been *living a good life* had she not died when she did.[38] This suggests that the destruction of her work could not be bad for Ann fifty years after her death. But this is a chit-chatty statement of my account that assumes the truth of hedonism; it does not accurately capture what DMPT entails when combined with axiologies of the sort Silverstein has in mind. As I've noted earlier in this chapter, DMPT is compatible with priorism, and with the axiologies typically endorsed by priorists, such as desire satisfactionism. So DMPT is compatible with the view that it is intrinsically good to have one's desire for posthumous admiration satisfied. As we saw in Section 1.3, there are different answers that might be given to the question of *when* the satisfaction of such a desire is intrinsically good; it might be good at the time of the admiration, or at the time of her desire for admiration. DMPT is compatible with both views. It entails that the destruction of Ann's work is bad for Ann at all those times when things would have been going better for her had the destruction not occurred. That might be before she died, or fifty years after her death—even though she would not have been living a good life at that time if the destruction had not occurred. Contrary to my chit-chatty gloss, DMPT does not require a person to be *living a good life* at a time in a counterfactual situation in order for an actual event to be bad for her at that time; according to some axiologies, things can be going well for someone at a time without that person being alive then. Of course, I have also argued in Chapter 1 that such axiologies are deeply problematic. But they are still compatible with DMPT.

[37] Silverstein (forthcoming), 9–10.
[38] For example, this is the gloss of my view I give on p. 1 of Bradley 2004, to which Silverstein is responding. Also see the second paragraph of this chapter.

Another objection to DMPT is based on a complaint about my use of language. There are a couple of ways the argument might go. First, one might think the locution 'E is bad for S at t' is completely made-up, a philosopher's construction. We do not ordinarily talk about things being bad for people at times. We talk about things being bad for people; we talk about the times at which bad things happen; we talk about the times the bad effects of an event happen; but we do not say in addition that harmful events are bad for people at those later times. And one might wonder what the point is of making up this locution. We can say everything we want to say by talking about things being bad, and talking about the times the bad things and their effects happen. The 'bad-for-at-a-time' language just makes things more mysterious.[39]

But we do talk in this way sometimes. We say that a person's smoking in his youth will cause him harm, and make him worse-off, later on. This is completely unmysterious. When we say things like this, we seem to be employing the bad-for-at-a-time locution. In any case, even if the locution 'E is bad for S at t' is made-up, we might think of it as a sort of shorthand for something like 'at t, S is worse-off than she would have been, in virtue of E's occurrence.' We say such things about ordinary evils all the time. The Epicurean challenge is to show that we can sensibly say such things about death.

This leads to a related objection. One might say that while my proposal gives a sense to the locution 'E is bad for S at t,' the sense I have given to it does not correspond to any ordinary way of using that locution.[40] Using the locution in its ordinary sense, nothing can be said to be bad for a person at a time when that person does not exist. Here is an analogy. Someone might offer a definition of the locution 'x kicks y at t' that makes it possible for the following statement to turn out true:

The Nixon sentence. Nixon kicked JFK at 7pm on January 23, 1979.

Perhaps the definition would entail that the Nixon sentence is true provided that Nixon moved his foot in a certain area, and that JFK

---

[39] Bill FitzPatrick suggested a worry along these lines.

[40] This objection has been raised, in different forms, by Fred Feldman and an anonymous referee.

would have been there had he existed.[41] We would not think that the definition shows it is possible to kick someone who does not exist, any more than we would think it possible to show that dogs have five legs by calling a tail a leg. Rather, we would think that the person is talking about some concept other than kicking, and giving it the same name.

Similarly, it may be argued, DMPT fails to provide a view that is relevant to traditional questions about the evil of death. Epicurus wanted to know whether death can harm the one who dies; DMPT provides a way to understand claims about harming the dead in a way that makes them come out to be true, but Epicurus and other ancient philosophers did not understand the claims in the way I suggest. Using words like 'harm' and 'bad' in their conventional senses, it is just as impossible to harm those who do not exist as it is to kick them.[42]

Perhaps it is true that, given the ordinary meanings of terms like 'harm' and 'bad,' something cannot be bad for a person at a time when that person does not exist. I do not know how to resolve this question about language, but I do not think it is necessary to do so. If it is true that the ordinary meanings of these terms preclude their use in the way I suggest, then we should revise our ordinary use of these terms. The question of whether death is genuinely bad for people cannot be resolved by an appeal to ordinary uses of words. If saying that death harms people after they die is not metaphysically problematic, this revision should not be scary. It is simply taking the ordinary way of talking about harms like toe-stubbings—which, if I am right, are bad for us at times after they happen—and applying it to death. The worry here is not a *semantic* one. If there is a worry, it is a *metaphysical* worry about an axiological property: how can death be bad for a person at a time if the person is not located at that time?

This brings us back to the Epicurean worry. Epicurus claimed that death cannot be bad for its victim at any time. I have claimed

---

[41] I thank Fred Feldman for the example.

[42] In Bradley 2004 I defended DMPT against this objection by pointing out a disanalogy between kicking and harming. Jens Johansson has argued that my response was unsuccessful (Johansson 2005, 83–5). I think Johansson is right.

that death is bad for its victim after she dies. Why think this answer is unavailable? One reason might be a general metaphysical principle: nothing can have *properties* at a time unless it is located at that time.[43] An alternative is a more restricted principle: nobody can have a *well-being level* at a time unless she is located at that time. If either of these principles is true, then a dead person has no well-being level to be compared to her well-being level at the closest world where her death does not occur. And if this were so, subsequentism in general would have to be rejected. We would have to either (i) endorse one of the alternative views, such as priorism, despite its drawbacks; or (ii) deny that death is bad for people at times, and thereby make death out to be a very different sort of evil from other evils of deprivation. We need not abandon DMPT if this were true, since as noted, DMPT is compatible with priorism. But much of the appeal of DMPT would be lost if subsequentism were untenable.

3.5 The Value of Nonexistence

3.5.1 *Zero or undefined?*

We must now determine the answer to what seems to be a rather obscure question: what is the well-being level of a dead person? In formulating DMPT, I have assumed that the answer is *zero*. DMPT requires us to compare two things: (A) S's well-being level at a time t at a world where S is alive at t, and is therefore located at t; and (B) S's well-being level at t at a world where S is dead at t, and thus not located at t. I have assumed that (B) is always zero.

But many philosophers think that a person has no well-being level—not even zero—at times after she has died. Some, such as Steven Luper, claim that this is 'obviously' the case.[44] I find it hard to see how it could be obvious whether dead people have welfare levels of zero or simply fail to have welfare levels at all.[45] One explanation

---

[43] For discussion of a similar principle see Holtug 2001, 370, and Bykvist 2007, 343.

[44] Luper 2007, 247.

[45] In other contexts, disputes about zero-value quantities versus no-quantities can be very tricky. See Balashov 1999 for discussion of examples from physics.

of why someone might think dead people have no well-being levels is that they are thinking of well-being in a different sense, as involving physical and emotional health.[46] A dead person is not maximally unhealthy, or at a midpoint between good and bad health; he simply lacks health altogether. But well-being in the sense relevant here is not the same thing as physical and emotional health, even if those things are related in some way to well-being. In this section I will look at some arguments that might be given for the view Luper calls obviously true; I will argue that dead people in fact have a welfare level of zero; and I will argue that even if Luper *et al.* are right, we can still accept subsequentism.

First, let me state the alternatives more clearly, so that we can see what is at stake. As stated in Section 1.2.1, one of the things a theory of personal well-being should do is to identify the value atoms, or the states of affairs that have basic, non-derivative intrinsic value for a person. We might say that the basic-intrinsic-value-for-S function, IV_s, takes states of affairs as arguments and yields numbers as values; the hedonist says that IV_s maps S's pleasure states to positive numbers, and maps S's pain states to negative numbers. The hedonist might add that S's overall welfare level at a world is the sum of the values of IV_s for all states obtaining at that world, and that S's welfare level at a time is the sum of the values of IV_s for all states obtaining at that time.

But this leaves open what the hedonist should say about states that are not S's pleasure or pain states, and in particular states obtaining at times at which S is not located. There are two possibilities for such states; they can be mapped to zero (the Zero View), or they can be left undefined (the Undefined View).[47] (Of course, there are also intermediate views according to which some are undefined while others are mapped to zero.) In defending DMPT I have assumed the Zero View. But defenders of the Undefined View insist (feet

According to Balashov, zero-quantities are not mere absences. 'They are respectable properties in the same sense in which their non-zero partners are' (254).

[46] Thanks to Simon Keller for this suggestion.

[47] The Undefined View is incompatible with Feldman's 'completeness' principle about basic intrinsic value; see Feldman 2000a, 332–3.

stomping, fist pounding) you just cannot have a welfare level at times at which you are not located![48] Not even zero! The Zero View is incoherent! As Silverstein says:

> Suppose, for instance, that, using a scale from +10 to −10, A calculates correctly that his average A-relative value level (e.g., his average happiness level), if he continues living, will be +2. What the Epicurean view claims … is that A cannot coherently use such a calculation as the basis for a prudential choice between life and death, since, as no value on the scale (including 0, the 'midpoint' value of neutrality or indifference) can intelligibly be assigned to A's death, there is nothing against which the value +2, however 'rationally' derived, can intelligibly be weighed.[49]

More recently, Silverstein claims that 'just as nothing can be good or bad for her *at a time that she does not exist*, so nothing can be indifferent for her *at that time*.'[50] Silverstein seems to think this is obviously true. But this is merely an assertion. So let us turn to the arguments.

3.5.2 Arguments for the undefined view

Silverstein suggests an argument in his discussion of an example given by David-Hillel Ruben:

> Suppose that someone now (in 2000) is eulogizing Napoleon … and consider the question: '*When* does Napoleon exemplify the property of being eulogized?' The puzzle is that (a) since the eulogy is occurring in 2000, the 'natural' answer to this question seems to be 'in 2000'; yet (b) Napoleon does not exist in 2000—and how can A exemplify properties at a time when A himself does not exist? … My solution … [is] to say that the question 'When does A exemplify property P?' is inapplicable where P is a posthumous property. Specifically, my response to the question about Napoleon is: Napoleon lived from 1769 to 1821; he is being eulogized in 2000; and that's the whole

---

[48] Silverstein 2000, 119; Bigelow, Campbell, and Pargetter (1990, 120); Draper (2004, 95); and Hershenov (2007) are among those who hold this view. Draper is much more circumspect in his (1999): 'I would need to be convinced that we cannot sensibly speak of the dead as occupying a level of well-being' (Draper 1999, 404).

[49] Silverstein 1980, 410. Silverstein has recently reaffirmed this line of argument (Silverstein 2000, 119).

[50] Silverstein (forthcoming), 11; his emphasis.

truth about 'when' in this case. There *is* no further question as to 'when' Napoleon exemplifies the property of being eulogized.[51]

This is a puzzling response to the question. Silverstein must be making heavy weather over the word 'exemplifies,' because he is happy to say that Napoleon is being eulogized in 2000, but not that Napoleon exemplifies the property of being eulogized in 2000. I wonder what the difference between these two claims is supposed to be. If the first is true, the second seems true too.

Perhaps the argument is that it is problematic to say that something can exemplify a property at a time when it does not exist.[52] Since we are assuming the truth of eternalism, it is less misleading to put the claim in the following way: nothing can exemplify a property at a time without being located at that time. ('How can A exemplify properties at a time when A himself does not exist?') DMPT evidently entails this problematic sort of property exemplification. But I cannot see why *Silverstein* thinks this is a problem. After all, Silverstein thinks that the time during which A's death 'can be an object of A's negative feelings ... is the time during which A is alive.'[53] This seems to suggest that A's death exemplifies a property—namely, the property of being an object of A's negative feelings—at a time at which A's death is not located—namely, during A's life. So Silverstein does not really have a problem, *in general*, with things exemplifying properties at times at which they are not located.

The problem must really be with one property in particular: the property of *having a well-being level*. Many have claimed that this property can be had by something only at times at which it is located. What arguments can be given for this claim?

Bigelow, Campbell, and Pargetter claim that dead people can have no well-being level, because the assignment of the zero level is 'stipulated' and 'arbitrary.'[54] But the assignment of the zero level is neither stipulated nor arbitrary. It follows from the general account of how a person's well-being level at a time is determined. For example, if hedonism is true, pleasures and pains are the only value atoms. If you are not getting any pleasure or pain at a given time, your

---

[51] Silverstein 2000, 133 n. 13.   [52] See Hershenov 2007.
[53] Silverstein 2000, 131 n. 6.   [54] Bigelow *et al.* 1990, 120.

well-being level is zero at that time, whether you are located there or not. Other axiologies may yield different results—e.g., objectualist correspondence theories might entail that people have positive or negative well-being levels at times after they die (Section 1.3). Those results may be implausible, but the implausibility is based on axiological intuitions, rather than metaphysical ones.

Steven Luper claims that 'it is obviously impossible to make any sense of a state of affairs' having a certain value (whether intrinsic or extrinsic) for a person during some time if that person is dead during that time. People are no longer responsive—they are incapable of valuing—when dead.'[55] But it is not clear why the *capacity to value* at a time t is necessary for having a well-being level at t, and no reason is offered to think it is. Luper defines responsiveness more carefully (and differently) as follows: 'I say that a creature is "responsive" at *t* if and only if its well-being may be affected at *t*—rising if certain conditions are met, and falling if certain other conditions are met.'[56]

Luper's argument seems to go as follows:

L1. If x has a well-being level at time t, then it is possible at t for x's well-being level to rise or fall.

L2. If x is dead at t, it is not possible for x's well-being level to rise or fall at t.

L3. Therefore, if x is dead at t, then x has no well-being level at t.

What we say about this argument will depend on what exactly is meant by 'possible' or 'may.' I assume that when Luper says a thing's well-being may be affected at t, he does not mean that it is *metaphysically possible* that the thing's well-being is affected at t. If that were what he meant, L2 would clearly be false. Currently, human beings lack the capability to revive dead people. Once you're dead, you're dead for good. (There are cases where people claim to have died and come back—I will not pass judgment about exactly what has happened in such cases.) But it seems possible that we'll solve the permanence problem. Maybe it will be possible to revive a dead person only in cases where the death has only recently occurred, and

---

[55] Luper 2007, 247.   [56] Luper 2007, 244.

where the brain and other important organs are sufficiently intact. Suppose scientists find a way to revive such people. I presume that once such a person is revived, it will be possible for his well-being level to be positive or negative. So long as this is metaphysically possible, which it surely is, we have a counterexample to L_2.

Luper must have in mind a more restrictive notion of possibility, such that even though it is metaphysically possible to affect the well-being level of a dead person, it is not possible in the relevant sense. This sense may be tied to the notion of *capacities*. A dead person lacks the *capacity* to feel pleasure or have desires, even though she *could* do so if she were revived. But the notion of capacity is elusive, and it is hard to see how to characterize it in a way that will get the results Luper wants. For example, it cannot be that merely the fact that external intervention is required in order for the person to feel pleasure entails that the person does not have the capacity for pleasure. For this could be the case with a living person as well—say, in the case of a person who has been knocked unconscious, or who is comatose—and there seems to be no reason to say that any living person lacks a well-being level.

Furthermore, no matter what we mean by a 'capacity,' I see no reason to think that a person could not have a *permanent* well-being level of zero, and that the level could not (in some suitably restrictive sense of 'could not') rise or fall given the person's inherent capacities. Suppose hedonism is true. Imagine Marsha is born without the capacity to feel pleasure or pain, and never develops that capacity;[57] imagine Greg is born with that capacity, but due to his circumstances, he never actually feels any pleasure or pain. Given Luper's account of responsiveness, Marsha is relevantly like a shoe—she has no well-being level at all—while Greg has a well-being level of zero. This just seems wrong. It seems better to say that both have a well-being level of zero, and that, unfortunately for Marsha, her well-being level will never rise nor fall no matter what the circumstances. It must remain at zero forever, or (to avoid begging questions) at least as long as she exists. Perhaps I could be convinced otherwise, but surely

[57] See Schroeder 2004, 33 for examples of people who have lost the capacity to experience pleasure and pain as the result of surgical procedures.

an argument is necessary. The problem raised does not depend on the supposition that hedonism is true; the example is easily adaptable to other axiologies (imagine someone who cannot form desires, and someone who can but never does ...). So supposing Luper has a more restrictive notion of possibility in mind, L2 is true, but L1 is false.

There is no obvious interpretation of Luper's argument according to which both premises are true. But a vexing question remains: what is the difference between a dead person and a shoe, such that a dead person can have a well-being level but a shoe cannot?[58] Surely something resembling Luper's notion of responsiveness is required to make this distinction. In calling a thing responsive, we are making a claim about its modal features: we are saying it is the sort of thing that *can be benefited or harmed*. So perhaps the difference between a dead person and a shoe is this: a person who is dead at t nevertheless has a positive or negative well-being level at some time, at some possible world. The same cannot be said of a shoe, which seems to be the sort of thing that could not possibly have a welfare level. Here, then, is a proposal for a necessary condition on responsiveness:

> R: Person S is responsive at time t only if there is some world w and some time t_n such that S has a positive or negative well-being level at $<w, t_n>$.

This much weaker condition for responsiveness seems more plausible than Luper's, since it gets the right results in the case of Marsha and Greg. R also rules out the possibility that shoes may have well-being levels, assuming common-sense opinion about the modal properties of shoes. Most importantly, R is compatible with dead people being responsive and having a zero well-being level. In order for his argument against subsequentism to work, Luper must provide some reason to prefer a more restrictive notion of responsiveness.

Here is another possibility. One might think that to be responsive at a time requires having some phenomenal state at that time, and to

---

[58] Thanks to Jens Johansson for pressing me on this point. In fact I think it may be completely harmless to attribute a zero well-being level to a shoe. As I show in Section 3.5.5, the distinction between zero well-being and no well-being is a distinction with no import.

have zero well-being level is to have phenomenal states but no good or bad ones. But this seems too restrictive. People lack phenomenal states at many points during their lives. It seems wrong to say that a person lacks a well-being level at such times. I suspect similar problems will befall other attempts to give a more restrictive notion of responsiveness.

3.5.3 Is well-being intrinsic?

Why, then, should we think a person cannot have a well-being level at a time without being located at that time? It is not because a person cannot have any properties at all at such times; the example of Napoleon's eulogy is just one example of this. It is not because the person lacks relevant capacities at that time; there seems to be no reason to distinguish a person who lacks a capacity from one who has it but never exercises it. And it is not because the person lacks phenomenal states, since every living person lacks phenomenal states at many times during her life.

A more promising line of argument appeals to the distinction between intrinsic and extrinsic properties. One might argue that a thing can have an intrinsic property at a time only if it is located at that time. Certainly many of the paradigmatic intrinsic properties are location-entailing. Mass and shape, for example, cannot be had by something at a time unless the thing is located at that time.[59] One might claim that, furthermore, well-being is an intrinsic property. Thus, the argument goes, nothing can have a well-being level at a time without being located at that time, just as nothing can have a shape at a time without being located at that time. (What was my shape in 1850? Surely I did not have any shape at all.)

But there are many theories of well-being, such as desire satisfactionism, according to which how well someone's life goes depends on whether certain things happen outside her body. The intrinsic property proposal would force us to reject all such theories; indeed, it

---

[59] Whether shapes are intrinsic is now controversial; see Skow 2007.

would force the rejection of all correspondence theories of welfare.[60] Of course, as we saw in Chapter 1, there are independent reasons to reject such theories. But they should not be ruled out by *fiat*. Certainly nobody who has argued for the Undefined View has intended their argument to be incompatible with correspondence theories of welfare.

But I reject correspondence theories. In Chapter 1 I argued for a hedonistic theory of well-being. And being pleased is, plausibly, an intrinsic property. So it might seem that, unlike most people, I am committed to saying that well-being is an intrinsic property. Is this a problem? I do not think that it is. When I am sitting in a chair and having no pleasant or painful experiences, I have a well-being level of zero. But this is not because of any pleasure or pain I am feeling then, nor in virtue of any other paradigmatically intrinsic property I have then. It's not, for example, in virtue of my body having the property of *being shaped like someone sitting in a chair* that I have a well-being level of zero. Rather, it's because I *lack* certain intrinsic properties.[61] I lack the property of being in pain, and I lack the property of being pleased. This—perhaps in conjunction with my satisfying the responsiveness requirement R, in light of there being some time at some world at which I feel pleasure or pain—is what, on hedonistic grounds, explains my zero well-being level.

If this is correct, then it seems entirely possible for a being that is not located at a time to have a zero well-being level at that time, for one way to have a zero well-being level at a time is to lack certain properties at that time. (Not the only way, because someone might have pleasures and pains at the same time that balance out.) An entity

---

[60] One might argue that while a person's particular well-being level is extrinsic, *having a well-being level at all* is intrinsic. But I take it that if a determinable property is intrinsic, then its determinates are intrinsic as well. Particular well-being levels are determinates of the determinable *having a well-being level*. So this response does not work. Anyone who thinks *having a well-being level* is intrinsic must reject correspondence theories of well-being. Thanks to Mikel Burley and Andre Gallois for discussion of this point.

[61] For a similar argument see Holtug 2001, 381. For a response to Holtug, see Bykvist 2007, 342–5. As far as I can tell, Bykvist's response applies only in cases where an individual never exists, not in cases where a person goes out of existence.

can lack intrinsic properties at a time without being located at that time. If there's one thing nonexistent objects are good at, it's lacking properties.

But this is too quick. It would seem that the 'negative' property, *not being pleased*, is an intrinsic property too, if being pleased is intrinsic. Not being pleased seems to satisfy the leading criteria for intrinsicness; it is, for example, shared among all duplicates (there is no set of duplicates, one of whom has the property of not being pleased while the other lacks it), and it can be had by something whether that thing is lonely or accompanied.[62] In general, it seems that if F is an intrinsic property, then lacking F is an intrinsic property too. So my well-being level while sitting in the chair is determined by intrinsic properties I have at that time: lacking pleasure and lacking pain. If this is right, then if I have a well-being level at a time at which I am not located, it must be at least in part because of some intrinsic properties I have then. Is *this* a problem?[63]

It is a problem only if it is impossible for something to have an intrinsic property at a time at which the thing is not located. While this seems true of some paradigmatic examples of intrinsic properties, such as shape properties, it is not obviously true of other intrinsic properties. There are, for example, trivial intrinsic properties, such as the property of being either round or not. Is there any reason to think that something could not have such a property at a time at which the thing is not located? We might just as well say that everything has such properties at every time. Negative intrinsic properties are not paradigmatic examples of intrinsic properties. So we might as well say, of negative properties such as *not being pleased* or *not being in pain*, that a person can have such properties at times at which the person is not located. The claim that things cannot have intrinsic properties at times at which they are not located derives what force it has from the paradigmatic examples, like being square or having a mass of 50 kg. It is unclear what justifies generalizing from these paradigmatic examples to the more obscure cases of trivial and negative intrinsic properties.

[62] See Lewis and Langton 1998, and Weatherson 2007 for more on intrinsicness.
[63] Thanks to Jens Johansson and Andre Gallois for discussion of this point.

If this is right, then the hedonist can agree that something's well-being level at a time is determined in part by its intrinsic properties at that time, and also say that things can have well-being levels at times at which they are not located. Thus, I think that defenders of the Undefined View have so far failed to provide a convincing argument that a dead person cannot have a well-being level of zero.

3.5.4 *Mere existence and rational preferability*

I now turn to a positive argument for that claim that people have well-being levels of zero at times at which they are not located. The argument expands on some brief remarks made by Kai Draper.[64] There must be some state we can be in, when we exist, such that when we're in that state, we have a zero well-being level. Let us stipulate that when someone is in a coma, he has a zero well-being level. (If you think comatose people have non-zero well-being levels, or fail to have well-being levels, then feel free to change the example. It does not matter.) Now suppose Ishani drops an anvil on Kris's head tomorrow, and consider two possible futures for Kris. In one future, F_1, Kris dies instantly. In the other future, F_2, Kris goes into a comatose state, never regains consciousness, and dies in ten years. Insofar as Kris's own well-being is concerned, he should be indifferent between these two futures. He has no self-interested reason to prefer one to the other. I think it is reasonable to conclude from this fact that *Kris is exactly as well off in the comatose state as he would have been had he not existed.* Thus it must make sense to assign a well-being level to Kris at times when he is dead; otherwise we could not say that Kris is as well off in the comatose state as he would have been had Ishani killed him instantly.

Here is a somewhat more formal statement of the argument:

1. Insofar as Kris cares about his well-being it makes sense for him to be indifferent between F_1 and F_2.

2. If 1, then Kris's well-being level in F_1 = Kris's well-being level in F_2.

---

[64] Draper 1999, 404–5. Also see Nagel 1979, 2.

3. If Kris's well-being level in F_1 = Kris's well-being level in F_2, then it makes sense to assign a well-being level to a person at a time when he is dead.

4. Therefore, it makes sense to assign a well-being level to a person at a time when he is dead.

I do not see how anyone could reject Premise 3. Someone might reject Premise 1 (recall Silverstein's remark: 'A cannot coherently use such a calculation as the basis for a prudential choice between life and death'), but to reject Premise 1 involves claiming that Kris's preferences are irrational, which seems very implausible given the details of the case.

That leaves Premise 2. One might reject Premise 2 on the grounds that it presupposes a fitting-attitude analysis of well-being, since a claim about Kris's well-being level in two outcomes is alleged to follow from what attitudes it makes sense for Kris to have concerning those outcomes. Chris Heathwood has argued that such analyses fail in light of the *bias towards the future* (Section 2.3); he thinks it is rational to prefer a smaller future benefit to a greater past benefit.[65] But in the example given here, both alternatives are equally in Kris's future. So even if the rationality of preferring an outcome changes over time while the value of the outcome remains the same, it could still be true that *in this case*, where both alternatives are equally in the future, the rationality of preferring one alternative to the other tracks the values of the alternatives. There seems to be nothing affecting Kris's preferences here that would make us suspicious that his preferences are failing to track facts about his well-being.

David Hershenov rejects Premise 2 on the grounds that we are sometimes indifferent between alternatives even when we have *no well-being level at all* in either alternative. For example, Kris might be indifferent between two worlds such that he never exists in either; but one cannot have a well-being level at a world if one never exists there.[66] Merely possible people, he says, have no well-being level.

But this objection is unpersuasive. First, note that Kris is not a merely possible person. He is a real person, who occupies an office

<hr />

[65] Heathwood 2008.   [66] Hershenov 2007, 174.

across the hall from mine and has a dog named Ranger. What Hershenov must really mean is that a person who is merely possible *from the standpoint of a possible world* has no well-being level at that world. Thus Hershenov seems to be presupposing something like Lewis's indexical conception of actuality, and denying that actuality is an absolute matter.[67] This is tendentious, but let it pass. We may still wonder why Kris cannot have a well-being level of zero at a world at which he never exists. Hershenov gives no argument for this claim. It seems no more or less plausible than the claim that Kris cannot have a well-being level of zero at a *time* at which he is not located, which is of course the very question at issue. So Hershenov's claim about worlds does not seem helpful in resolving the dispute about times.

Suppose Hershenov is right, and it is possible to be prudentially indifferent between two alternatives without having a well-being level in each—perhaps because there are insuperable metaphysical difficulties associated with postulating that people have well-being levels at times at which they do not exist. Would this matter? I do not think so. To say that it makes a difference is to assign far too much axiological weight to mere existence. For it remains the case that from the standpoint of rational deliberation, *future nonexistence is, and should be, treated just like future existence with zero well-being.* So I could just reformulate DMPT, and all the other views in this book, as views about rational preferences, and get analogs of all my claims about death. For example, I could replace all instances of 'E is bad for S at t' with 'concerning time t, it is rational for S to prefer that E not occur.' Little of substance would be lost by this translation. In fact, we might well wish to introduce a new term, call it *well-being**, that corresponds to this concept of rational preferability. If you are happy to make the relevant claims about rational preferability, but not about value or well-being, then I advise you to imagine asterisks in the relevant locations as you read on.

So far, I have defended the following views about death's badness. Death is bad because (and when) it makes its victim's actual life worse than the life the victim would have had. It is bad to the extent

---

[67] Lewis 1986a, 92–6.

that the victim's life would have been better if the victim had not died. It is bad at all those times at which things would have been going better for the victim had her death not occurred. And it is bad at a time to the extent that things would be going better for the victim at that time than they would have been had her death not occurred. DMP and DMPT entail these views. Taken together, these views constitute a simple, plausible, and attractive account of death's badness. These views do not entail subsequentism; however, I have also argued that dead people have a zero well-being level, and that therefore death is bad for its victim at times after the victim has died. One may accept DMP and DMPT without this accretion, but as I've argued, DMPT-plus-subsequentism is more plausible, and yields a more unified picture of harm, than DMPT-plus-priorism. In the next two chapters I will consider some alternative views about the extent of death's badness.

4

DOES PSYCHOLOGY MATTER?

Die at the right time!

Friedrich Nietzsche, *Thus Spoke Zarathustra*

It is commonly thought that features of an individual's psychology—her memories, anticipations, and other mental connections to her past and future—are relevant to the badness of her death. If this were true, it would have implications for the evaluation of the deaths of beings such as babies, fetuses, and non-human animals; their deaths would be, in general, less bad than the deaths of typical adult humans. As we will see, it would also have implications for the Difference-Making Principle (DMP), which, you will recall, is the view that the overall value of an event for a person is equal to the difference between the value of her actual life and the value of the life she would have had if the event had not happened. In this chapter I will argue that the victim's psychology is not relevant in the way people have thought, and that the deaths of babies, fetuses, and animals may be very bad for them. I begin with the question: at what age is it worst to die?

4.1 When Is it Worst to Die?

Assume, for the sake of exposition, that life is worth living at every moment. How does the magnitude of the badness of a person's death for her change throughout the course of her life? Many views are

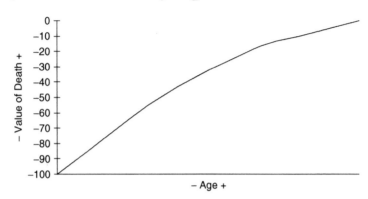

Figure 4.1

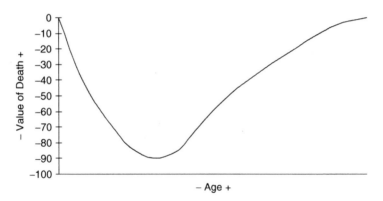

Figure 4.2

possible, but only two seem plausible to very many people (other than Nietzsche). Some think a person's death always gets less and less bad the older she gets, as in Figure 4.1.

Others think a person's death starts off not very bad, gets worse for a while, reaches a peak level of badness sometime around young adulthood, then starts getting less and less bad towards old age, as in Figure 4.2.

These views disagree about the relative badness of the deaths described in the following two cases:

Baby. A three-week-old baby, Baby, dies in an accident. Had Baby not died then, he would have enjoyed a happy childhood and adolescence, gone to college, entered a PhD program in philosophy, become a professional philosopher, and lived an enjoyable life until dying at age 80.

Student. A 23-year-old philosophy graduate student, Student, dies in an accident after a happy childhood and adolescence. Had Student not died then, he would have become a professional philosopher and lived an enjoyable life until dying at age 80.

DMP, by itself, does not tell us whether Figure 4.1 or Figure 4.2 gives the correct picture of the magnitude of the evil of death. It does not tell us whether Baby's death is worse than Student's. But given any remotely plausible theory of welfare, DMP entails that Baby's death is worse than Student's. There are some theories of welfare according to which Student's life contains some evils, as a result of his premature death, that Baby's life does not contain. For example, it is likely that Student has many more desires, and stronger desires, than Baby has, so Student's death causes more desire frustration than Baby's death.[1] But Student's life contains many desire satisfactions that Baby's life lacks; so, plausibly, Student's life is better than Baby's, even according to desire satisfactionism.[2] As long as Student's life is better than Baby's, DMP entails that Baby's death is worse, since their counterfactual lives are stipulated to be identical in value.

Jeff McMahan and Christopher Belshaw have argued that Student's death is worse, and that Figure 4.2 gives the correct picture of how bad death would be at the various stages of life.[3] In the next few sections I defend DMP and the picture in Figure 4.1, and I show that the views endorsed by McMahan and Belshaw face serious problems. I focus in particular on McMahan's 'Time-Relative Interest Account' of the evil of death (Section 4.4.2), according to which the magnitude of

---

[1] For an example of this line of argument, see Singer 1999, 310.

[2] For more discussion of desire satisfactionism and the value of death, see <http://peasoup.typepad.com/peasoup/2004/10/death_revisited.html>.

[3] McMahan 2002, 184; Belshaw 2005, 46. Also see Benatar 2006, 159.

the harm of death is determined in part by facts about psychological connectedness.

The resolution of this dispute has implications for topics of obvious practical significance. A principle that entails that Baby's death is much less bad than Student's might also entail that the death of a fetus is even less bad, or not very bad at all for the fetus; this would have implications for the moral permissibility of abortion. This is part of McMahan's strategy for defending the permissibility of some abortions; David DeGrazia claims that McMahan's arguments 'substantially advance the case for a liberal position' about abortion.[4] Another example concerns the allocation of medical resources. Societies face decisions about what portion of their resources they should devote to reducing infant mortality. Devoting resources to reducing infant mortality might require taking resources away from other projects that help save the lives of older people. One consideration that seems relevant to such decisions is the relative magnitudes of the harms at stake in the decision to allocate resources in one way rather than another. (Of course, other factors are surely relevant as well.) John Broome describes many other examples of situations that require some sort of weighing of the harms of deaths of people of different ages.[5] Anyone interested in these issues should be interested in the question about Baby and Student.

It is important to keep in mind a possible source of confusion in the evaluation of deaths. There is one way in which it might be argued that Student's death is much worse than Baby's: Student has put a lot of work into his future, and thus *deserves* that future much more than Baby does. And we might think Student's death is more tragic for this reason. But this is not to say that Student's death is worse *for Student* than Baby's death is *for Baby*. Rather, it is to say that even though Student's death is not as bad for Student as Baby's is for Baby, *the world* is made worse by Student's death than by Baby's death. The question DMP answers, however, and the question that is at hand here, is how bad death is for its victim, not for the world. This distinction will become important in Section 4.3.

---

[4] McMahan 2002, ch. 4; DeGrazia 2003, 442.   [5] Broome 2004, 1–18.

4.2 **The Cure**

McMahan presents a number of arguments against DMP. One is based on the following example:

The Cure. Imagine that you are twenty years old and are diagnosed with a disease that, if untreated, invariably causes death ... within five years. There is a treatment that reliably cures the disease but also, as a side effect, causes total retrograde amnesia and radical personality change. Long-term studies of others who have had the treatment show that they almost always go on to have long and happy lives, though these lives are informed by desires and values that differ profoundly from those that the person had prior to treatment.[6]

McMahan says that it makes sense to refuse the treatment in this case, given how little psychological connection there would be between one's present and post-treatment selves were one to receive the treatment. But DMP entails that it is better to receive the cure. The psychological disunity is irrelevant according to DMP.[7]

I think DMP gets the right result here. The decision to refuse treatment is shortsighted and irrational. It seems in many ways similar to the decision of a child to ignore the consequences of his behavior on his adult self, since he does not currently care about the things his adult self will care about. Perhaps some others will share my judgment. But not everyone will. So it is worthwhile to think about some possible sources for the judgment that it is rational to refuse the cure, and to determine whether, if the judgment is based on those sources, any problem is posed for DMP.

In the example, we are to suppose that if I take the cure, *I* will continue to exist through the changes in personality, memory, desires, and values. But these sorts of examples sometimes lead people to a psychological account of *personal identity*, not merely prudential concern. When McMahan says that if you received the treatment, in the future 'you would be a complete stranger to yourself as you

---

[6] McMahan 2002, 77.

[7] Of course, the discontinuity could be relevant if it causally affected the intrinsic value of the life in some way, such as by making it less pleasant. This is supposed to be ruled out in the example by stipulation.

are now,' he is very close to saying that psychological continuity is necessary for personal identity (though he explicitly denies that claim).[8] Someone in the position described in the example might well reason in the following way: *I think I'd rather take the cure and get the extra life. But I'm not entirely sure I would continue to exist after getting the treatment, given the psychological changes I would undergo. This depends on the truth about personal identity over time, and there is no consensus about what such identity amounts to. Better not to risk it.* If one reasons in this way, it is to doubt whether the future individual is the *same* individual that is the basis for the decision. In discussing a similar case, Belshaw says: 'What we want is for our own lives to continue, not for there to be some life or other, no matter how good, that starts where our own life leaves off.... It's bad for him to die, but it's bad, as well, to turn into someone else, or to become a person he cannot, now, much care about.'[9] McMahan and Belshaw are clearly *tempted* to say that the pre-cure individual does not survive, but is replaced by someone else. Surely others feel the same temptation. But to the extent that this temptation forms the ground for the judgment that it is rational to refuse the cure, there is no argument here against DMP. If receiving the cure causes the patient to go out of existence, DMP entails that benefits and harms accruing to the post-cure patient are not relevant to the evaluation of the life of the pre-cure patient.

Another reason one might choose not to receive the cure is that the details might make a difference. In particular, it might matter *in what respects* the patient's desires change as a result of the treatment. We often care about our future welfare even when we know that in the future we will desire things we currently do not desire; but our caring is limited. For example, I might reflect on the sorts of changes that people typically undergo as they age, or that my older relatives have undergone, and realize that I myself am likely to undergo similar changes. I might come to believe that I will become interested in playing golf, and that my politics will become more conservative. I might well take some golf lessons in the hope of making my future self happier, but refuse to contribute money to conservative political causes (or to save money for my future self to contribute to those

---

[8] McMahan 2002, 78.   [9] Belshaw 2005, 48–9.

causes) even though that would also make my future self happier. We might say that whether we should care about the desires of our future selves depends on whether those future selves will desire not only what we are currently not interested in, but also what we think is *bad*. If my future self will have different and (from my current perspective) worse moral values, I might choose not to be able to act on those values; this might be because I care about things other than my own well-being, or (perhaps in a more extreme case) it might be because I think I would not be well-off if I held such values, even if I were pleased.

There is another possible source of intuitive support for the idea that one should not receive the treatment. If one were to receive it, one's life might contain more valuable episodes, but it would lack unity. This might be even more obvious in the case of someone like the musicologist Clive Wearing, whose life seems to consist of millions of very short, unconnected experiences. Consider what McMahan says about this sort of case: 'While we may think that the experiences have value individually, it is less plausible to attribute independent value to them as a collection or aggregate.'[10] And recall that Belshaw says turning into someone else would be a bad thing.[11]

Both McMahan and Belshaw seem to think that, even if there is a single person surviving through the cure, and the parts of the person's life are good taken individually, the life taken as a whole is not so great. Perhaps such a disjointed life scores very low on the narrative unity scale. Since attributing value to lives on the basis of shape or narrative unity is compatible with DMP, DMP can give the results McMahan and Belshaw desire in these cases.[12]

To put the point another way, consider someone who judges that the treatment is not in her interests. She might decide, before the proposed treatment date, that the treatment is not in her best interests *then*. But she might also make the *time-neutral* judgment that a long,

---

[10] McMahan 2002, 76.   [11] Belshaw 2005, 49.

[12] McMahan also suggests that the weakening of prudential unity relations could be a misfortune in itself (McMahan 2002, 174). If what he means is that it is intrinsically bad for a person to have the prudential unity relations between her present and future selves weakened, then his suggestion can also be incorporated into DMP, providing yet another possible line of defense.

happy life interrupted in the way the treatment required would be less good for her than a shorter life without the treatment, and this might be the basis for the time-relative judgment.[13] In order to get an argument against DMP going, McMahan and Belshaw need to argue that the time-neutral judgment is not what's doing the work.

Some might find the cure unappealing because of the *way* in which one's desires and values change.[14] They change as a result of the medical intervention—not as a result of more ordinary processes like maturing and aging.[15] The new desires and values are, in a way, imposed upon the patient rather than arising naturally. Some might find such a life worse than a shorter one in which the desires and values arise as a result of ordinary processes, even though the change results from the patient's own decision to receive the treatment.[16] Again, McMahan and Belshaw need to argue that time-neutral judgments about the disvalue of having one's desires altered by a medical intervention are not driving the argument here.[17]

To recap briefly, there are several reasons not to receive the cure that are compatible with the truth of DMP. (1) Receiving the cure would cause the patient to cease to exist, and to be replaced by a different individual. (2) We care about more than our own well-being, and receiving the cure might be incompatible with other things we care about (e.g., doing what we now take to be the morally right thing). (3) One's lifetime welfare level is partly determined by certain sorts of psychological unity. (4) One's lifetime welfare level is determined not only by whether one's desires are satisfied, but also by the way in which they arose in the first place. (Note that one cannot accept all four explanations at once! But only one is necessary.) Since I think I am rationally required to take the cure, I do not endorse any of

---

[13] Thanks to Andre Gallois for putting the idea to me in this way.

[14] See Korsgaard 1989, 122–3. Thanks to Irem Kurtsal Steen for discussion.

[15] This consideration seems to be mitigated by the fact that it is the agent herself who is choosing to undergo the treatment and thereby have her desires changed.

[16] Thanks to an anonymous referee for suggesting improvements to this point.

[17] Another idea, which I will not pursue here, would be to say that while there is a single person who survives the cure, that person lives two lives. Perhaps this is the way Bernard Williams would describe the case; see Williams 1973, 92–4.

these responses; but those who think it is rational not to take the cure should consider whether they think so because they believe one of (1)–(4), rather than because they think DMP is false.

4.3 Abortion

The most serious problem McMahan sees for DMP is that it seems to entail that in typical cases, the worst possible time for a person to die is just after she comes into existence. In the following paragraph he targets this apparent implication of DMP:

> If identity [rather than psychological connectedness] were what matters, the worst death, involving the most significant loss, would be the death of an individual immediately after the beginning of his existence. But the loss that would have occurred if that individual had simply been prevented from beginning to exist would not have been significant at all. This is hard to believe. It suggests that it is profoundly important to prevent the existence of an individual who would die within seconds of beginning to exist.[18]

McMahan finds it hard to believe that it should matter so much whether a being fails to come into existence at all, or comes into existence only to die moments later. But DMP apparently entails that it does indeed matter a lot. McMahan thinks most people will agree that it does not matter, and cites as evidence the fact that most people are not extremely concerned to stop spontaneous abortions; if people really thought that earlier deaths were worse, they would view 'the vast number of spontaneous abortions that occur as a continuing tragedy of major proportions.'

Since this is McMahan's primary argument against DMP, it will be helpful to spell it out in some detail. As I see it, the argument goes something like this:

M1. If DMP is true, then death is extremely bad for its victim at the earliest stage of life.

M2. If death is extremely bad for its victim at the earliest stage of life, then it is extremely important to prevent someone from

[18] McMahan 2002, 165.

coming into existence if he would otherwise die just after coming into existence.

M3. It is not extremely important to prevent someone from coming into existence if he would otherwise die just after coming into existence.

Conclusion. Therefore, DMP is not true.

M2 should be rejected. Before I explain why, let me briefly touch on the other premises. M1 is true, provided that the victim's life would have been worth living. I can imagine someone taking issue with M3, in the following way: Coming into existence is a big deal in the life of an individual. Many things are true of a person after she comes into existence that were not true before. One of those things is that she can die. Another is that she can be harmed. Insofar as we care about preventing harm to people, then, we must think it is important to prevent someone from coming into existence if he would otherwise die shortly after coming into existence. Nevertheless, I do not wish to hang my hat on objection to M3. So I turn to M2, which requires detailed discussion.

Part of the rationale behind M2 is the claim that failing to come into existence is not bad for someone. If it were, then it would not much matter whether someone failed to come into existence or came into existence only to die shortly thereafter. Is it bad for a person not to come into existence? This is an interesting question. Suppose I'm considering some harms I might have suffered in the past. If I had died shortly after coming into existence, I would of course have been harmed. Suppose instead I had been prevented from coming into existence. McMahan says that would not have been bad for me, since in such a case, there would have been no subject of harm, no victim.[19] Thus McMahan presupposes that in order to be harmed (and perhaps to have any properties at all) at a world, one must exist at that world. But that's not obvious. We might wish to treat worlds like times. In Section 3.5 I showed that people can have

---

[19] Parfit also suggests that one cannot be harmed by being prevented from existing (Parfit 1984, 489). For good recent discussions, see Holtug 2001, and Bykvist 2007.

well-being levels at times when they do not exist. Perhaps people can also have well-being levels at *worlds* at which they do not exist. We might consider a world in which my existence is prevented, and say that a number of things are true *of me*—the actual me—at that world: e.g. that it's not the case that I exist, that it's not the case that I enjoy myself or have any knowledge. We might conclude that an event that brought about these sorts of negative facts about me would be harmful to me at that world, even though I never exist there.[20]

Note that this strategy would not account for an *actual* case where an act of contraception prevents a person from coming into existence (as opposed to a case where we take some actually existing person and imagine a world in which that person never existed), at least not without some additional metaphysical assumptions; for in such a case, there is no actual person we can point to and say that not existing would have harmed *her*. Is the merely possible person who would have existed but for the contraception actually harmed? Our options here depend on whether there are merely possible objects or not. Either way, there is no problem for DMP. First, suppose there are some merely possible, nonactual people. Then we can say, of the merely possible person who would have existed but for the contraception, that it is just as bad *for her* to be prevented from coming into existence as it is for her to die shortly after coming into existence. There is no great disparity between the two harms. (As will become clear, this would not commit us to saying that we have any obligation to bring such a person into existence.) On the other hand, suppose that there are no merely possible objects. Then there is no subject of harm here, and so there is still no problem for DMP, because there is no person such that DMP entails that it is a good thing for that person that she was prevented from coming into existence rather than dying shortly after coming into existence. Again, there is no great disparity between harms (in this case because

---

[20] Kris McDaniel argues for this point in greater detail in an unpublished manuscript. The point is of course not uncontroversial; Williams seems to deny it, saying that we 'cannot think egoistically' about such a situation (Williams 1973, 87).

there are no harms). So we do not get an undesirable result for DMP whether we admit merely possible objects or not.

Let us grant, however, that failing to come into existence is not bad for someone. Nevertheless, we may still reject M2, because M2 is true only if it is always important to prevent great harms, and it seems clear to me that it is not. Philosophers of all persuasions should agree on this, as I will now show.

First, we might make a distinction between the extent to which an event *harms an individual*, and the extent to which that harm *matters morally*. It is entirely consistent to say both that the death of an infant or a fetus harms it greatly and that the harm does not matter morally as much as harm to an adult.[21] To explain how this could be so, we might appeal to the notion of desert.[22] Perhaps a harm matters more morally when it is suffered by someone who deserved to be benefited than when suffered by someone who did not deserve any benefits. Or we might appeal to a notion of moral status. We might say that certain individuals have moral status, while others lack it, and that harms matter morally only when suffered by individuals with moral status; or perhaps that moral status comes in degrees, and that harms matter more when suffered by individuals with greater moral status.[23] (In fact, McMahan himself seems sympathetic to such ideas.[24]) If we hold such a view, we can reject M2.

Of course, not everyone finds notions like desert and moral status unproblematic. Consider a consequentialist who thinks that the permissibility of an action depends on the amount of intrinsic value produced by the action and its alternatives, where that intrinsic value is not determined in any way by facts about moral status or desert. Suppose this consequentialist accepts M1. Now suppose Gustaf finds himself in a situation where he can prevent the existence of someone who, were he to come into existence, would die immediately. Call that

---

[21] The view that how much a harm matters depends solely on its magnitude is endorsed, for example, by Don Marquis in his famous paper on abortion (Marquis 1989, 194).

[22] See, for example, Feldman 1992.   [23] Against this view, see Harman 2003.

[24] See his discussion of the 'Intrinsic Worth Account' and the 'Two-Tiered Account' of the wrongness of killing, and his discussion therein of the ideas of a 'threshold of equal worth' and a 'threshold of respect' (McMahan 2002, 243–65).

individual Krister. Here are Gustaf's alternatives, and the intrinsic values of the consequences for each individual affected:

Alternative	IV for Krister	IV for others	Total IV
a1 (prevent existence)	0	0	0
a2 (allow existence)	0	0	0

If Gustaf does a1, nothing bad happens to Krister, since Krister never gets to exist at all, so Krister never dies. If Gustaf does a2, Krister suffers a great harm; he dies immediately, and if that had not happened, he (we may suppose) would have lived a long and happy life. Nevertheless, the intrinsic value for Krister of each alternative is the same! No matter which alternative is performed, Krister gets zero intrinsic value. Thus the consequentialist has no reason to favor one of these alternatives over the other. The consequentialist should say that when comparing two actions, *it does not matter* whether one of the actions causes an event that is harmful to someone while the other does not; the intrinsic values of the two outcomes are all that matter.[25]

It might seem surprising that consequentialists should say that harms do not matter. But in fact everyone, consequentialist or not, should agree about this. Remember that death is a harm that is merely *extrinsically* bad for its victim. Death is harmful because of what it prevents; it has a sort of extrinsic value. When determining whether there is any reason at all not to perform the action, we should never consider the extrinsic values of the results of the action. For example, suppose you save my life by curing me of a debilitating disease, and as a result I live an extra ten very happy years. I then die from an unrelated cause, and my later death deprives me of yet another ten happy years. Your saving my life caused my later death, and my later death was very bad for me; but my later death was merely *extrinsically* bad, and in evaluating how good it was that you saved my life, the extrinsic badness of my later death is irrelevant.[26] Before my death I would not be justified in complaining: *yes, you saved my life and gave me ten happy years, but you also caused an event that will prevent me from getting another ten happy years; so the bad you caused cancels the good*

---

[25] Thanks to Neil Feit for discussion of this point.
[26] Thanks to an anonymous referee for the example.

you caused. The reason this would be an unjustified complaint is that your saving my life, rather than letting me die, did not prevent me from getting those later ten years of a happy life that my later death prevents me from having. Similarly, in the case at issue in McMahan's argument, the act of allowing a person to come into existence, rather than preventing his existence, does not prevent that person from getting the goods of which his death deprives him. Even though the act of allowing the person to come into existence causes another event that is very harmful to the person, that fact is not relevant to the evaluation of the act.

Thus M_2 depends for its plausibility on two principles. One is controversial: that failing to come into existence is not bad for someone. The other is false: that it is important not to cause harmful events (i.e., extrinsically bad events) to occur. It is important not to cause an extrinsically bad event to occur only when, in so doing, one is causing something intrinsically bad to happen or preventing something intrinsically good from happening. For example, it is important not to cause a person's death because in so doing, one is preventing that person from receiving some intrinsic goods. This is not the case in McMahan's example, since allowing someone to come into existence only to die shortly afterwards does not cause any intrinsic evils or prevent any intrinsic goods. So even if death is worse the earlier it occurs, we might have no obligation to prevent very early deaths from occurring by, say, preventing doomed conceptions from occurring. In light of the falsity of this principle about harm, we must reject M_2.

So McMahan's main argument against DMP is unsound, and the argument based on *The Cure* is inconclusive at best. But even if I have shown that these arguments are not decisive against DMP, I have not shown that DMP is superior to views that entail that Student's death is worse than Baby's. I now turn to examining those views and why they fail.

4.4 Desires and Time-Relative Interests

To find a way in which Student's death is worse than Baby's, we must find some important way in which Student and Baby differ. But not only that: it must be a difference that cannot be incorporated into DMP. That is, it must be shown that, *even though Student is deprived of less of a good life than Baby*—even though Student's actual life is better than Baby's actual life—Student's death is worse. This is important to remember. One difference between Baby and Student is that Student has invested a great deal of time and effort into seeing to it that his future goes a certain way, while Baby has not. Student's death renders those investments futile. Another difference is that Student's life has begun to take a certain sort of shape or narrative; the narrative of Baby's life has not yet really begun. Student's death gives his life a very bad shape, or a tragic narrative, while Baby's death just results in his life having no real shape or narrative at all.[27] DMP can account for both of these differences between Baby and Student, as long as it is intrinsically bad to have one's investments rendered futile or to have a life with a bad narrative structure. And if those things are not intrinsically bad, why think they are relevant to the evil of death?

If the best theory of personal welfare entails that it is so bad to have one's investments rendered futile, or to have a life with tragic narrative structure, that Student's life turns out to be worse than Baby's, then DMP would yield the result that Student's death is worse than Baby's. It seems very implausible to me that the best theory of well-being would entail that Student's life is worse than Baby's, and to my knowledge no such theory has ever been defended. But my concern in this chapter is merely to defend DMP, not to argue about the theory of welfare.

4.4.1 What we want when we die

Another important respect in which Baby and Student are different is that Student has fully formed desires about his life. At the time of his death, he wants the future he would have had. Baby does not have any such desires, at least not about his future beyond the next few minutes. As noted at the beginning of this chapter, this does not by

---

[27] McMahan takes both the investment facts and the narrative facts to be relevant to the value of death (McMahan 2002, 183).

itself make Student's death worse, since Baby's death deprives Baby of many satisfactions of not-yet-formed desires. But we might take deprivations of satisfactions of not-yet-formed desires to be irrelevant to the value of Baby's death. Here is what Belshaw says about a case much like Baby and Student:

Alice [the teenager] herself is already looking forward to, and planning for this future, has already made an investment in and commitment to this upcoming life. It's what she wants. Ben [the baby], of course, is hardly yet able to think beyond his next meal .... In this sense the ending of his life, no matter how good it will be, doesn't represent a loss to him.[28]

Belshaw never states the view he is putting on the table, but here is a simple view that is suggested by his remarks: how bad it is for a person to die depends on, at the time of the person's death, how much the person *wants* the future he would have had, rather than its *value* for the person.[29] If this view were true, Baby's death would be much less bad than Student's. But this is unacceptable. Consider a depressed teenager who commits suicide. At the time of her death, she likely does not desire the future she would have had. But her death is still very bad for her. The problem is that people sometimes do not desire what is really good for them, and in those cases, what seems relevant to the evaluation of their deaths is what would really have been good for them, not what they want (except insofar as just getting what one wants is good).

An obvious fix to this problem would be to take not the person's actual desires at the time of death, but rather some idealization of those desires—perhaps the set of desires the person would have were she subjected to a course of cognitive psychotherapy, or possessed and entertained all relevant information about the possible futures available to her. But we face an uncomfortable dilemma. Either the idealized desire set contains appropriate desires (i.e. desires of the right strength) for what is really good for the person, or it does not. If the latter, the view will get the wrong results, e.g. in the case of

---

[28] Belshaw 2005, 46.

[29] McMahan agrees that a person's desires at the time of his death are relevant to the value of his death (McMahan 2002, 183). But he says that other factors are relevant as well.

the depressed teenager. If the former, the view will get the same results as DMP, and in particular will entail that Baby's death is very bad—the very result the view was supposed to avoid. For on that assumption, Baby's idealized desire set will contain desires for all the future goods his death takes from him.[30]

Perhaps a clever person could get around these sorts of problems. I am skeptical. In any case, Belshaw himself does not really seem to endorse the view that how bad it is for a person to die depends on her desires at the time of death. Rather, he thinks it is facts about psychological connectedness that are really important: 'Although it's bad for young children to die, then, we might with reason think it's less bad than a similar death for an older child, or an adult. Why? Because there's not the same degree of psychological connectedness, or integration, running through their lives.'[31] Belshaw seems to be endorsing something like McMahan's 'Time-Relative Interest Account' (TRIA), which is inspired by Parfitian considerations about psychological connectedness. I now turn to that view.

4.4.2 *The time-relative interest account*

According to DMP, the value of a death is determined by facts about the values of lives. The time-relative interest account (TRIA) is different in one way that seems superficial: according to TRIA, the value of a death is determined by facts about 'interests.' Interests are not desires; they are to be understood in terms of well-being. What is the relationship between interests and well-being? One's interests, according to McMahan, 'reflect what would be better or worse for one's life as a whole'; for one to have an interest in something is 'to have a stake in it' or 'for one's well-being to be engaged with it.'[32] These remarks do not make clear exactly what McMahan takes the relation between interests and well-being to be. I will assume that he thinks that something is in a person's interest if and only

---

[30] For a detailed discussion of these issues see Boonin 2003, 70–9. Boonin's concern is not the same as mine, since he is concerned with the right to life, and I am here concerned only with axiology.

[31] Belshaw 2005, 46.   [32] McMahan 2002, 80.

if it is intrinsically good for that person; or, in language closer to McMahan's, a person has an interest in something if and only if she has egoistic reason to care about it. On the other hand, 'one's present time-relative interests are what one has egoistic reason to care about *now*.'[33] A person's present time-relative interests can diverge from his interests *simpliciter* provided that the *prudential unity relations* holding between his present and future selves are weak—i.e., provided that his present self has less egoistic reason to be concerned about his future self than about his present self.

Of course, if the prudential unity relation relates an individual at time t_1 to an individual at time t_2 to the degree to which the identity relation holds between those individuals, then since identity does not come in degrees, one's interests and one's time-relative interests would never diverge. McMahan argues that the prudential unity relation is not identity, but psychological unity. (Here McMahan's view is in the spirit of Parfit, who says, 'personal identity is not what matters.'[34]) My current time-relative interest in some future event depends, in part, on the extent of psychological unity between myself now and myself in the future. Psychological unity comes in degrees, so interests and time-relative interests can differ in strength. To determine the extent of psychological unity over time, we ask questions such as these: how much of the person's psychology (beliefs, desires, etc.) remains the same? How rich is the person's mental life? To what extent does the future person remember things that happened to the past person? Does the future person make attempts to satisfy the past person's desires?[35]

Thus the extent to which an event such as an individual's death is (instrumentally) bad for her depends not only on how (intrinsically) bad its effects are for her at the time the effects occur, but on the strength of the psychological unity between the individual at the time of the instrumentally bad event and at the time of the event's bad effects. When the connection is not strong, the intrinsic value of the effects is multiplied by a fraction corresponding to the strength of the connection—the weaker the connection, the smaller

---

[33] McMahan 2002, 80.   [34] Parfit 1984, 217.
[35] McMahan 2002, 74. Compare to Parfit 1984, 284–5.

the fraction.[36] Mere physical continuity of the brain—even without any strong psychological connections—is sufficient for a non-zero level of time-relative interest.[37]

Given that background, here is how McMahan states the relevant parts of TRIA:

We cannot, I have argued, assess how bad it is for a person to die simply by ascertaining how much better his life as a whole would have been if he had not died when and how he did…. In addition to asking how much good a person's future life would have contained, we must also ask…. How close would the prudential unity relations have been between the individual as he was at the time of his death and himself as he would have been at those later times when the goods of his future life would have occurred? … The badness of the loss must be discounted for the absence of [psychological connections].[38]

When we try to state TRIA more carefully, it turns out to be a fairly complicated view. But the basic idea is easy to illustrate with a picture, so let me begin there. Let the solid line in Figure 4.3 represent the value of Jan's life over time, as it would have gone were she to have lived her full lifespan. Suppose she were to die at t_5. Had Jan not died then, her life would have continued to be worth living for its duration; she would have received many pleasant experiences until her later death at t_9, and those experiences would have been good for her. However, the psychological connections between Jan at t_5 and Jan at the times of the pleasures would have grown increasingly weaker, such that the loss of the pleasures at the end of her life would have represented a much smaller loss to Jan at t_5. As McMahan might say, it is almost as if the pleasure she would have gotten would be received by someone other than the person who exists at t_5 (though someone she cares about a lot). The dotted line represents the t_5-relative value of Jan's life over time. If TRIA were true, the badness of Jan's death would be determined by the area after t_5 beneath the dotted line, rather than the area beneath

---

[36] McMahan 2002, 80.

[37] McMahan 2002, 79. This is in contrast with Parfit, who says 'it would not matter if my brain was replaced with an exact duplicate' (Parfit 1984, 285).

[38] McMahan 2002, 183–4.

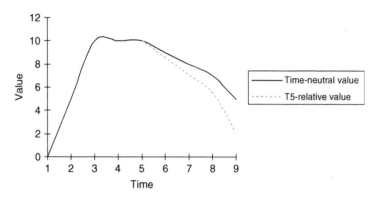

Figure 4.3

the solid line. So her death comes out less bad according to TRIA than it does according to DMP.

Now that you have the basic idea, let me formulate the view more carefully. It is best formulated in two parts. First, there is a part that tells us, for any actual or possible event, and any time t, the extent to which a person has a t-relative interest in that event occurring. Let us introduce a piece of technical jargon here that will make the view easier to state: the extent to which a person has a t-relative interest in an event occurring will be called the *t-relative interest value* of the event for the person.[39] Here is what seems to be McMahan's account of t-relative interest value:

> TRIA1. The *t-relative interest value* of an event E for subject S = the intrinsic value of event E for subject S, multiplied by a fraction corresponding to the level of psychological unity between S at t and S at the time of E.[40]

TRIA1 is just a definition of a piece of jargon. It does not provide us with an account of the *overall value* of anything—i.e., the value

---

[39] Thanks to Neil Feit for suggesting this terminology.

[40] In the case of merely possible events, I presume that the fraction corresponds to what *would have been* the level of psychological unity between S at t and S at the time of E had E occurred.

something has for a person taking into account not only its intrinsic value for that person, but also its value in virtue of what it brings about and prevents for him. Thus TRIA1 does not provide a way to evaluate deaths; TRIA needs a second principle that gives us the overall value of an event for a person based on the time-relative interest values of other events for that person. Given that someone's death causes and prevents certain events, and given the t-relative interest values of those events (for some t), how do we determine the value of that death for its victim? McMahan does not answer this question. I tentatively suggest the following simple principle:

> TRIA2. The overall value of an event E, occurring at time t_1, for subject S = (the sum, for every event E^* caused by E, of the t_1-relative interest value of E^* for S) minus (the sum, for every event E^* caused *not* to occur by E, of the t_1-relative interest value of E^* for S).[41]

The idea here is to incorporate into a single value both the time-relative interest values of the good and bad things E brings about, and the time-relative interest values of the good and bad things E prevents from coming about. In stating TRIA2, we must choose a time to which to relativize the interests, and we must choose a way to determine the overall value of an event based on the values of its various consequences. The simplest way to determine overall values is to add and subtract values in obvious ways, much like in DMP; I do not think the arguments that follow rest importantly on this decision. The choice of a time to which to relativize the interests will be a point of contention shortly. But for now, let us tentatively take TRIA to be the conjunction of TRIA1 and TRIA2. Whether this is McMahan's view or not (and we will soon see reasons to think that McMahan's view is substantially more complicated than even this complicated view), it seems like a view worth considering.

(An exegetical tangent addressing a possible source of confusion: Sometimes McMahan writes as if he is not giving an account of the badness of a death for a person *simpliciter*, but rather an account of

---

[41] For simplicity's sake I am ignoring the intrinsic value of the event itself; this is harmless in this context since all parties agree that death has no intrinsic value.

the badness of a death for a person *at a time*. Consider, for example,
the following passage: 'When the prudential unity relations that
would bind an individual to himself in the future would be weak,
death matters less *for that individual at the time*.'[42] This suggests
that TRIA does not say anything about how bad death is overall for
someone *simpliciter* (i.e. not relative to any time).[43] Thus Broome says,
understandably, that we must think of TRIA as giving an account of
'badness for the person, relative to that particular time.'[44] Were this
the correct way to understand TRIA, it might forestall some of the
criticisms to come. In many passages, however, McMahan makes no
mention of relativity to a time; for example: 'Notice, however, that
it seems reasonable to want one's own death to be less bad—to be a
lesser rather than a greater misfortune.'[45] Here there is no mention
of wanting the death to be less bad at some particular time, such as
when it occurs. I think TRIA is best construed in the second way—as
making a claim about non-time-relative overall values of events for
people. The time-relativity McMahan really seems concerned about
comes in TRIA$_1$, where the time-relative interest value of an event
for a person is determined on the basis of when that event occurs,
not in TRIA$_2$, which gives the overall value of an event for a person
simpliciter based on the time-relative interest values of some other
events. If TRIA were merely making a claim about the time-relative
overall values of events for people, it would not be a competitor to
DMP at all, and a large portion of McMahan's book would be a *non
sequitur*.)

Assume that a three-month-old baby is not strongly connected
psychologically with its adult self. We can get TRIA to yield the
result that Student's death is worse than Baby's, provided that the
multiplier for psychological unity is sufficiently small in the case of
Baby. In Figures 4.4 and 4.5, we see how this works. According to
TRIA, the magnitude of Baby's death at t$_2$ is determined by the area

---

[42] McMahan 2002, 172, emphasis his.

[43] Earl Conee, in comments at the Creighton Club, suggested that this is
a more plausible interpretation of McMahan's view, especially in light of the
objection I raise below. However, McMahan confirmed in conversation that he
indeed intends TRIA to be a view about the non-time-relative badness of death.

[44] Broome 2004, 249.   [45] McMahan 2002, 172.

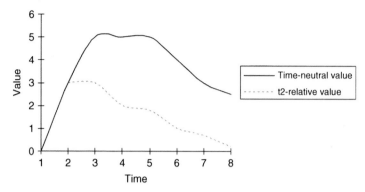

Figure 4.4 (Baby)

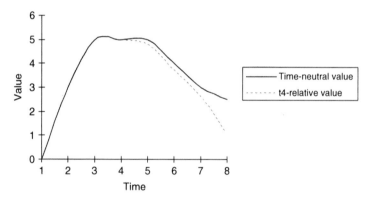

Figure 4.5 (Student)

after t2 under the dotted line in Figure 4.4, while the magnitude of Student's death at t4 is determined by the area after t4 under the dotted line in Figure 4.5. The solid line represents the value of each life over time as it would have been had the death not occurred.

Here are some other relevant implications of TRIA. (1) TRIA gets the results McMahan wants in *The Cure*, since the patient would not be very strongly connected psychologically pre- and post-treatment. (2) TRIA entails that it is not very bad for a person to die just after coming into existence, since at such an early stage, the person would have few psychological connections with his future adult self. (3) TRIA entails that the deaths of 'lower' animals, such as cows, are not as bad as the deaths of typical human beings, even if their deaths deprive them of similar amounts of goods, since cows apparently lack strong psychological connections with their future and past selves. Many will regard this as a point in favor of TRIA. I will have more to say about cows in Section 4.5.

4.4.3 *Objections to TRIA*

However, TRIA must be rejected. Consider this example. Suppose Claire has an infant son Charlie, who has a trust fund that he may use when he turns 25. For simplicity's sake, suppose, sadly, that the trust fund is the only potential source of happiness in Charlie's life. Claire intends to drain the fund secretly, and prevent Charlie from ever finding out about its existence. Let t_1 be the time when Charlie is three weeks old, and let t_4 be the time when he is 23 years old. Does it matter whether Claire steals the money at t_1 or t_4? It is very hard to see how it could possibly matter, but if TRIA is true, the harm of the theft depends on when it occurs. Were Claire to leave the money alone, Charlie would have had a much better life upon turning 25; the theft would deprive him of some goods, and the time-neutral intrinsic value of those goods for him would be the same no matter when she steals the money. But by TRIA1, the t_1-relative interest value of those goods for Charlie would be less than the t_4-relative interest value of them for him, given that the psychological connections between his three-week-old self and his 25-year-old self are much weaker than those between his 23-year-old self and his 25-year-old self (see Figure 4.6). So by TRIA2, we get the result that the early theft would be less bad for Charlie than the later one. That is clearly wrong.[46]

Furthermore, TRIA will face problems with events that occur before a person exists yet still manage to harm the person. Consider

---

[46] Broome gives a somewhat more complicated counterexample that seems to target the same feature of McMahan's view (Broome 2004, 251).

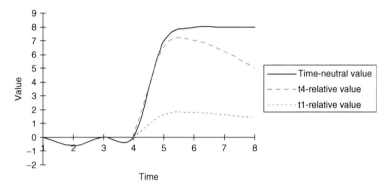

Figure 4.6 (The Trust Fund)

a version of the trust fund case in which the trust fund for Charlie exists, and is drained by Claire, *before* Charlie exists. TRIA seems to entail that Claire's draining the fund is not harmful to Charlie at all, since there are *no* psychological connections of any sort between Charlie in his twenties and before he exists. (There is not even physical or functional continuity between parts of Charlie's brain at those two times, since he lacked a brain when he did not exist.) But of course it is harmful to him.[47]

McMahan is aware of this sort of problem. He discusses a similar argument against TRIA: 'If the Time-Relative Interest Account implies that it would be less objectionable to cause a person to be sterile by injuring him when he was a fetus than to cause him to be sterile by injuring him later, say at age fifteen, this is seriously damaging to the account's credibility.'[48] He gives this response to the argument:

In short, the objection assumes that, if we are to explain why the infliction of prenatal injury is wrong by reference to the victim's time-relative interests, we must focus on only those time-relative interests that the victim has

---

[47] For a defense of the claim that an event occurring before a person exists can harm that person, see Feldman 1991, 219.

[48] McMahan 2002, 282. One potential complication here is that McMahan is discussing the wrongness of inflicting harm, rather than the badness of the occurrence of an event.

prenatally, at the time the act is done. But that restriction is arbitrary; we must evaluate the act in terms of its effect on all those time-relative interests it affects, present or future.[49]

If we apply this reasoning to the trust fund case, the idea seems to be that the early theft is just as harmful as the later one, since the early theft, like the late one, frustrates Charlie's time-relative interest in having the money *at the time he would have received it.*

This response suggests that TRIA, as formulated, does not capture McMahan's view. I have assumed, in TRIA2, that in order to determine the value for a person of an event that takes place at time t_1, we look at the t_1-relative interest values for the person of all the goods and evils caused and prevented by the event. I made this assumption because McMahan explicitly says that when someone *dies* at time t_1, it is the t_1-relative interest values of the goods and evils prevented by the death that are relevant to evaluating the death. But this seems to be only because of special features of death cases. McMahan seems to think that in other cases not involving death, there are times t, distinct from t_1, such that the t-relative interest values of those goods and evils are also relevant. What is the guiding principle here? Is there a principle that gives us the results McMahan wants—that Baby's death is less bad than Student's, that it is rational to refuse the cure, and that stealing Charlie's trust fund is equally bad for Charlie no matter when the theft occurs? That is, in determining the value of an event, to what time(s) do we relativize the values of the goods and evils it causes and prevents? Which time-relative interest values are relevant? Unfortunately, it is not exactly clear what McMahan's view is; even more unfortunately, when we attempt to get a view going that avoids the trust fund objection, things get more complicated in a hurry. (Readers with low tolerance for complicated views who have hung in this far may wish to skip ahead to Section 4.5.)

Recall that McMahan claims that 'we must evaluate the act in terms of its effect on *all those time-relative interests it affects*, present or future.'[50] McMahan seems to be denying that we relativize to a single time; rather, we relativize to *all* times. That is, the value of an

---

[49] McMahan 2002, 283.   [50] McMahan 2002, 283, my emphasis.

event E is determined by the t-relative interest values, *for all t*, of the events caused by E. This suggests the following revision to TRIA$_2$:[51]

> TRIA$_2'$. The overall value of an event E for subject S = (the sum, for every event E* caused by E, *and every time t*, of the t-relative interest value of E* for S) minus (the sum, for every event E* caused *not* to occur by E, *and every time t*, of the t-relative interest value of E* for S).

Let TRIA$'$ be the conjunction of TRIA$_1$ and TRIA$_2'$.

TRIA$'$ requires us to add a lot more numbers than does TRIA.[52] (It is also much more difficult to represent with a graph.) Perhaps it gets the right result in the trust fund case, since there will be many future times at which Charlie will have time-relative interests in getting the money. But it fails to get the results McMahan wants in *The Cure*. After receiving the cure, the patient would receive a lot of goods, and there would be many post-cure times *t* such that receiving those goods has a high *t*-relative interest value for the patient. So if TRIA$'$ is true, the decision to receive the cure has a very high value for the one who gets it, and refusing the cure is bad overall.

We might be able to distinguish *The Cure* from the trust fund case by adopting a version of *actualism* about interests. The general idea would be this. When one decides to refuse the cure, one is deciding not to have one's interests changed in a certain way. The interests one would have had, had one taken the cure, *are not one's actual interests.* Hence, their counterfactual satisfaction or frustration does not affect the value of one's actual choice to refuse the cure. Whether the choice is a good one is determined only by one's actual interests.[53] In the trust fund case, on the other hand, stealing the money frustrates some of Charlie's actual future interests, and frustrates the same ones no matter when the theft occurs.

---

[51] David DeGrazia suggested a view along these lines as an interpretation of McMahan.

[52] For the purposes of this chapter I suppose that time is discrete, since if time were continuous, TRIA$'$ and its descendants would face devastating problems involving infinite value; even ordinary cases would involve adding and subtracting infinities.

[53] In personal correspondence McMahan has suggested that this is his view.

Distinguishing actual from possible interests is a tricky matter
in this context. Recall that interests, according to McMahan, are
not desires; to say that something is in my interest is to say that
it enhances my well-being. The problem is: how could it be the
case that something actually fails to enhance my well-being, but
would enhance my well-being if things had gone differently? Some
things are only contingently good for me: doing crossword puzzles,
for example, might actually be good for me, but not be good for
me if I failed to enjoy it. But that is because doing crossword
puzzles is only extrinsically good for me. It is good for me because
it makes me happy. Death is not bad because it prevents us from
getting extrinsic goods; it is bad because it prevents us from getting
intrinsic goods. So the real problem is: how could it be the case that
something is *intrinsically* good for me given one outcome, but not
given another outcome? On many accounts of well-being, this idea is
simply incoherent. Suppose pure hedonism were the correct account
of well-being, for example; how could an experience of pleasure be
intrinsically good for me *only contingently*? If pure hedonism is true,
it is necessarily true.

There is one account of well-being that allows for the sort of
actualism McMahan wants: the *objectualist version* of preferentism
or desire satisfactionism (see Section 1.3).[54] Recall that according to
this view, if someone intrinsically desires that P, and P obtains, P's
obtaining is itself intrinsically good for that person. For example,
suppose I intrinsically desire that the Yankees win the World Series.
Then if the Yankees do indeed win, the fact that they win is intrinsically good for me; it is in my interest. But that fact is good for
me only contingently, since, had I not desired that they win, their
winning would have failed to be intrinsically good for me. On
this view, 'interests' are to be understood as the objects of intrinsic desires, and the value of a state of affairs for me is *relative to
a world*.

Given this account of well-being, and given the introduction
of world-relative intrinsic value, we need to redefine time-relative
interest value. I propose the following definition:

---

[54] See Rabinowicz and Österberg 1996, and Bykvist 1998, 64–5.

TRIA₁*. The *t-relative interest value* of an event E for subject S *at world w* = the *w-relative* intrinsic value of event E for subject S, multiplied by a fraction corresponding to the level of psychological unity between S at t *at w* and S at the time of E. (In the case of merely possible events, the fraction corresponds to what *would have been* the level of psychological unity between S at t and S at the time of E had E occurred.)

And I propose the following account of the overall values of events for people:

TRIA₂*. The overall value of an event E for subject S *at world w* = (the sum, for every event E* caused by E, and every time t, of the t-relative interest value of E* for S *at w*) minus (the sum, for every event E* caused *not* to occur by E, and every time t, of the t-relative interest value of E* for S *at w*).

Let TRIA* be the conjunction of TRIA₁* and TRIA₂*.

Here is how TRIA* works in *The Cure*. Add the following details to the story: I actually am a Yankees fan and do not care about hockey, but if I were to take the cure, I would become a hockey fan, and would want the New York Rangers to win the Stanley Cup. So if I were to receive the cure, it would be intrinsically good for me if the Rangers won, but were I to refuse, it would not be. Suppose I refuse the cure at time t_c. At time t_r ($t_r > t_c$) the Rangers win the Stanley Cup. The t_c-relative interest value of the Rangers' winning for me, *at the actual world*, would be zero. So I would, in essence, be deprived of nothing in virtue of the Rangers' winning, even though, if I had taken the cure, their winning would have been intrinsically good for me. According to TRIA*, whether refusing the cure is good for me depends on (i) how many other things would have happened that would have been in my *actual* interest, and (ii) the extent to which the values of those goods are discounted in virtue of the diminished psychological connectedness that would have obtained between myself at t_c and myself at the time I received the goods. Since many of the things that would have been in my interest were I to have taken the cure, like the Rangers' winning, are not in my actual interest, and since the discount for lack of psychological connectedness is high in this case, TRIA* seems to entail that refusing the cure is good for me.

TRIA* also seems to get the right results in the trust fund case, since the same time-relative interests are frustrated no matter when the theft occurs.

But TRIA* faces new problems. First, it presupposes a view about well-being that very few people have ever held, whereas DMP is compatible with every theory of well-being. Further, it should be clear that the view about well-being presupposed by TRIA* will be subject to the sorts of objections I raised in Chapter 1, especially the problem of well-being and time. If the Rangers' winning is intrinsically good for me, and I die before they win, their winning seems to be good for me at times after I have gone out of existence (assuming internalism). Thus my well-being could rise posthumously based on what happens in the Stanley Cup playoffs. This is a major cost to be borne by TRIA*, and an important advantage for DMP.

TRIA* yields some other bizarre results. For one thing, it entails that whether an event would be good for someone might depend on whether the event occurs or not.[55] Consider *The Cure*. I explained how TRIA* seems to entail that refusing the cure would be good. But this was on the assumption that I actually refuse the cure. If I were to accept the cure, then my actual desires would be different. I would actually desire that the Rangers win the Stanley Cup, and so their winning would be intrinsically good for me. So it seems that TRIA* might well entail that, were I to (actually) receive the cure, my (counterfactual) refusal would have been bad for me. Thus, in *deliberating* about whether to take the cure or not, one important thing I will have to consider is *whether I will in fact take the cure or not*. I cannot evaluate which choice is better without knowing what I will in fact do. This is an unacceptable consequence of TRIA*.

This problem is a result of TRIA*'s actualist presuppositions. Moving from actualism to necessitarianism could solve the problem.[56] Instead of restricting the relevant interests to actual interests, or

---

[55] This problem mirrors one for certain versions of consequentialism pointed out by Erik Carlson (1999, 256–7). Carlson attributes the point to Wlodek Rabinowicz.

[56] For more on actualism and necessitarianism (but as concerns people rather than interests), see Arrhenius, 'The Moral Status of Potential People' (manuscript).

what is actually intrinsically good for someone, we would restrict the relevant interests to *necessary* interests; we would look at what her interests would be, what would be intrinsically good for her, *no matter what happens.*[57] But necessitarianism is little better than actualism. Suppose Mikey has no interest in trying a certain sort of cereal, but Jane says to him: 'Try some. You'll like it.' Mikey tries it, and likes it. As a result of his decision to try the cereal, he desires that he be eating that cereal, and since he's eating it, his eating it seems to be intrinsically good for him. But according to necessitarianism, his decision to try the cereal was not good for him at all. He could have chosen not to try it, in which case eating it would not have been in his interest. So eating the cereal is not necessarily good for him; thus, even though his decision to try it causes him to have an interest in it, the satisfaction of that interest is irrelevant to the evaluation of the decision to try it.

TRIA and the proposed revised versions of it either fail to get the results McMahan wants in these cases, or are unacceptable on independent grounds. And there are more problems too. TRIA also faces a complication involving some intrinsically valuable events that last a long time. Consider an event E that lasts from time t_1 to time t_2, where E is intrinsically good for subject S. Suppose that the psychological connections between S at t_1 and S at t_2 are very weak. And suppose that the intrinsic goodness of E cannot be explained by appeal to the intrinsic goodness of its temporal parts, because E has some global feature that is intrinsically valuable. TRIA$_1$ does not tell us, for any time t, how to determine the extent of S's t-relative interest in E. TRIA$_1$ tells us to look at the psychological connections between a person at one time and that person at another time when something intrinsically good or bad happens to her. The fact that E is such a long event makes that impossible; for many times t during E, the psychological connections between S at t and S at t_1 will be different from the psychological connections between S at t and S at t_2.

This example schema is not merely an abstract possibility. It is commonly held that narrative structure, or the 'shape' of a person's

[57] In personal correspondence McMahan suggests he endorses necessitarianism.

life, is a component of personal well-being.[58] Facts about narrative structure are facts about someone's life taken as a whole. Among the value atoms, on this view, are whole lives—the value of the whole is not reducible to the value of its parts taken in isolation. Psychological connections between a person at the first moment of life and that person at the last moment of life are very weak. So we cannot use TRIA₁ to determine the time-relative interest value for a person of his whole life. TRIA₁ is incompatible with the view that narrative unity is intrinsically valuable.

As in the Trust Fund, McMahan is aware of a potential difficulty in this neighborhood. His response to the problem is as follows:

> During that period within a life when the prudential unity relations are strong (and in most cases this period stretches from childhood through old age), what an individual has most egoistic reason to want, at any given time, will be what would be best for his life as a whole, and this will be importantly affected by considerations of narrative unity. As I noted earlier, when the prudential unity relations are strong, a person's time-relative interests coincide with his interests.[59]

McMahan seems to be saying that at most times t during a person's life, the value of the person's life for her will be the same as the t-relative value of the life for her. This is because the prudential unity relations are strong for most of a person's life. But it is not clear exactly how this response is supposed to work. The prudential unity relation relates a person at one time with that person at another time; in order to apply TRIA to a particular case, we need to know which two times to look at, so that we can determine the degree of psychological unity between the person at the first time and the person at the second time, and get a multiplier for prudential unity. When using TRIA to determine the time-relative value for a person of the narrative unity of his life, at which two times should we look? The first time would be the time to which the value of the intrinsically valuable event is relativized; the second time would be the time of the intrinsically valuable event. The problem

---

[58] For example, see Velleman 1993, and MacIntyre 1981.
[59] McMahan 2002, 176.

with narrative unity is that we cannot fill the second term of the relation.[60]

This problem arises only for those who think that there are irreducibly 'global' facts that help determine the intrinsic values of lives, such as facts about narrative structure. I reject such views. McMahan accepts them, though for reasons independent of his reasons for endorsing TRIA.[61] He could hold on to TRIA and deny that narrative structure affects well-being, but many would take this to be a significant cost of TRIA.

There is more room to wiggle here.[62] Perhaps McMahan could hold some sort of 'averaging' view, according to which in the case of an event for a person occurring at time t_1 that causes a long event with irreducibly global intrinsic value, the discounting multiplier is determined by taking all the specific times t during the event, determining the discounting multiplier for each such time by looking at psychological connections between the person at t_1 and t, and taking the average of those multipliers. (Momentary events would just be a limiting case.) Or McMahan could say that there just is no discounting in the case of long events, that it is only momentary goods that are discounted. (But why?) There are many other possibilities. I will refrain from speculating about which route is best, and simply note that if we accept DMP, we need not worry about such complications.

Surely there is some kernel of truth in the vicinity of TRIA that has attracted thoughtful philosophers. It does seem true that at any given time t, a person values more highly those goods that are in store for him at times when he will be closely psychologically connected to himself at t than those goods in store for him at other times. Call this the *bias towards psychological sameness*. We all have this bias simply in virtue of the fact that continuity of desire

[60] Note that the objection is not simply that TRIA does not explicitly account for narrative structure; if that were the objection, TRIA could simply be regarded as incomplete, to be supplemented with an additional principle. The objection is that TRIA is *incompatible* with the intrinsic value of narrative structure; the view blows a fuse if narrative structure is relevant to well-being.

[61] McMahan 2002, 174–6.

[62] Thanks to Earl Conee for suggesting some possible defenses of TRIA.

is one of the determining features of psychological unity. Suppose I now desire that the Democrats win the elections in 2028, but in 2028 I will desire that the Republicans win the elections in 2028. This means the level of psychological connectedness between me now and my 2028 self is less than one. Right now, I will of course value more highly the satisfaction of the my current desire; I might not now value the satisfaction of my 2028 desire at all. But it is unclear what follows from this fact. The bias towards psychological sameness seems irrational. Its existence is easily explained by the fact that we are motivated by desires we actually have right now, not by desires we will have in the future but do not presently have.

Furthermore, even if the bias towards psychological sameness were rational, nothing would follow straightaway about the overall values of events for people, as we saw in the discussion of the bias towards the future in Section 2.3. If the arguments I've just given succeed, then we should deny that the overall value of an event for a person is determined by facts about psychological connectedness; so if the rationality of preferring the occurrence of some event is determined by facts about psychological connectedness, it follows that the value of an event does not always track the rationality of preferring (at some time) the occurrence of that event. How rational it is to prefer a given event is not necessarily proportional to the overall value of that event.

I have tried to show that DMP can get around the problems McMahan and Belshaw raise, and that views that are compatible with Student's death being worse than Baby's, such as TRIA, face serious problems of their own. I conclude that DMP is more plausible than TRIA, and that a person's death gets less and less bad the older she gets; thus, Baby's death is worse than Student's. Of course, there might be some other view that could account for the view that Student's death is worse without encountering the sorts of problems detailed here, but I think I have at least given good reason to be skeptical about the possibility of developing a plausible view that entails that Student's death is worse.

4.5 Cows

I have shown that facts about a person's psychological unity relations over time do not make a difference to how bad her death is for her. But there are other ways in which facts about an individual's psychology may be thought to affect the badness of her death. David Velleman claims that cows cannot conceive of themselves as existing through time, and that it follows from this fact that their deaths are not bad for them. Velleman holds the following thesis about intrinsic value: 'unless a subject has the bare capacity, the equipment, to care about something under some conditions or other, it cannot be intrinsically good for him.'[63] Given this thesis and the supposition that cows cannot conceive of their futures, it follows that cows have no lifetime well-being at all. For cows cannot care about how their whole lives go; they can care at any given time only about how things go for them at that very time. And since cows have no lifetime well-being levels, their deaths cannot be bad for them.

The argument is somewhat more complicated than this, because Velleman holds a bifurcated view about well-being, according to which momentary well-being is wholly different from lifetime well-being (see Section 1.3). Lifetime well-being is not reducible to momentary well-being or to facts about the arrangement of bits of momentary well-being.[64] Lifetime well-being is determined (at least partly) by facts about *narrative unity*—whether early sacrifices pay off later in life, and so on. Momentary well-being is determined by facts about that particular moment, e.g. facts about one's experience at that moment. Thus well-being is 'radically divided.'[65] Velleman does not deny that cows have momentary well-being. But he still thinks death cannot be bad for a cow.

Here, then, is Velleman's argument:

There is no moment at which a cow can be badly off because of death, since (as Lucretius would put it) where death is, the cow is not; and if there is

---

[63] Velleman 1993, 354–5.   [64] Velleman 1993, 343–6.
[65] Velleman 1993, 345.

no moment at which a cow is harmed by death, then it cannot be harmed by death at all. A premature death does not rob the cow of the chance to accumulate more momentary well-being, since momentary well-being is not cumulable for a cow; nor can a premature death detract from the value of the cow's life as a whole, since a cow has no interest in its life as a whole, being unable to care about what sort of life it lives. Of course, a person can care about what his life story is like, and a premature death can spoil the story of his life. Hence death can harm a person but it cannot harm a cow.[66]

Velleman's argument is complicated, but I take it the argument goes like this:

V1. If death is bad for a cow, then either death is bad for a cow at some particular moment, or death detracts from the lifetime well-being level of the cow.

V2. In order for something to be bad for a being at a moment, that being must exist at that moment.

V3. If V2, then death is not bad for a cow (or a human) at any particular moment.

V4. Therefore, death is not bad for a cow (or a human) at any particular moment (from V2, V3).

V5. Cows cannot conceive of themselves existing through time.

V6. If cows cannot conceive of themselves existing through time, then cows have no lifetime well-being levels.

V7. If cows have no lifetime well-being levels, then death does not detract from the lifetime well-being level of a cow.

V8. Therefore, death does not detract from the lifetime well-being level of a cow (from V5, V6, V7).

V9. Therefore, death is not bad for a cow (from V1, V4, V8).

The only uncontroversial premise here is V7. V3 and V5 are questionable and require further argument. V2 and V6 are false. Thus Velleman's conclusions are unjustified and, I think, false as well.

Let us start with V5: 'Cows cannot conceive of themselves as existing through time.' One might wonder where Velleman gets his

[66] Velleman 1993, 357.

information about cows. Temple Grandin and Catherine Johnson have argued that cows and other non-human animals have much more interesting mental lives than people have thought.[67] I am confident that many non-human animals can conceive of themselves as existing through time. But let us suppose, for the sake of this argument, that Velleman is right about the mental lives of cows. Even if he is wrong about cows, there are probably some other animals that cannot conceive of themselves as existing in time, and Velleman's argument would be relevant to those animals.

V_3 is true only if there is no time when an individual exists at which that individual's death can be bad for him. As we saw in Section 3.3, a widely held position is that death is bad for its victim at particular moments while that individual is alive: namely, those moments at which the individual had interests that were later frustrated by her death. I think this view is false, so I am happy to accept V_3, but those who accept the Feinberg/Pitcher account of death's badness cannot accept it.

I argued extensively in the last chapter that V_2 is false. Velleman here is endorsing Epicurus' argument from Section 3.1, according to which death is not bad for its victim before the victim dies, because the death has not occurred yet, and is not bad for its victim after the victim dies, because the victim no longer exists then. But as I have argued, death is bad for the victim at all those moments at which the victim would have been living a life worth living had she not died when she did—at all the moments at which she would have had positive momentary well-being.

But even if my arguments from Chapter 3 succeeded, Velleman would still be able to give an interesting argument that death is not bad for a cow. Suppose a cow's death may be said to be bad for it at certain moments after its death. Still, if a cow has no *lifetime* well-being level, then its death cannot be bad for it *overall*. Cows do not have lifetime well-being levels, according to Velleman; well-being is not 'cumulable' for cows, since they lack the capacity to care about extended periods of their lives. If death is bad in virtue of making its victim's whole life worse than the life she would have lived, death

---

[67] Grandin and Johnson 2005.

is not overall bad for any individual whose actual and counterfactual lives lack intrinsic value altogether. So we must turn our attention to V6, which is really where the action is.

According to V6, a necessary condition for an individual to have a lifetime well-being level is that the individual can conceive of itself as existing through time, and therefore can conceive of its life as a whole. V6 is supported by the following principle about intrinsic value, which I'll call the Capacity to Care Condition:

> CCC: Nothing can be intrinsically good or bad for an individual unless the individual has the capacity to care about it.

Cows can care about what happens to them at a moment, but since they lack the capacity to see themselves as temporally extended beings, they cannot care about extended periods of their lives, or their whole lives. So if CCC is true, extended periods of cows' lives have no intrinsic value for them.

The claim that extended periods of a cow's life have no intrinsic value for the cow has bizarre implications. Consider two possible futures for a cow. In one future, the cow is tortured constantly until it dies. In the other future, the cow is happy and free. Which future is better for the cow? If Velleman is right, neither future is better. The second future has better moments for the cow, but *on the whole, it is no better or worse than the first future.* That cannot be right.[68] Velleman claims that given the truth of CCC, 'any method of combining the values of a cow's good and bad moments will be purely arbitrary and consequently defective.'[69] But could it really be arbitrary to suppose that when we combine the values of a cow's bad moments, the moments of torture, the result is as good as, or better than, the result of

---

[68] There is an alternative line of argument that one might give. One might argue that since a cow lacks the ability to conceive of its life as a whole, cows are not temporally extended entities. Rather, at each successive moment there is a new individual, psychologically unconnected to past and future individuals but causally connected to them. There is no individual that is composed of these instantaneous cow-slices. If so, then there is no such thing as 'lifetime well-being' for a cow that is distinct from momentary well-being, since no cow lives more than an instant. I take it this is not Velleman's view, so I will not evaluate it here.

[69] Velleman 1993, 356.

combining the values of the cow's good moments? Surely at least some methods of combining values can be seen, intuitively, to be wrong.

We must, then, reject the claim that a cow's life has no intrinsic value for it, and must therefore reject CCC. But there must be some reason Velleman finds CCC to be plausible. I think there is a principle in the neighborhood that is more plausible, that perhaps captures what Velleman had in mind, but that is compatible with the claim that cows have lifetime well-being levels.

In his discussion of the value of punishment, G. E. Moore noted a difference between the value of something *on the whole* and the value of something *as a whole*.[70] When a wrongdoer is justly punished, the punishment involves pain (or some other intrinsically bad thing, such as loss of freedom) inflicted upon the wrongdoer. That pain is bad in itself. However, the pain is part of a larger whole consisting of the wrongdoing and the punishment. That larger whole has a kind of positive value, because its parts fit together in a way that seems appropriate—more appropriate than a whole consisting of someone acting wrongly and then enjoying the fruits of the wrongdoing. The combination of the wrongdoing and the punishment, then, has value *as a whole*. Something's value *as a whole* is the value it has in virtue of its irreducibly global features, the relations between its parts. When something has value as a whole, it has a kind of value that is not reducible to the values of its parts—it is a value atom. Velleman and several others have claimed that a life that starts badly and improves is better than a life that starts well and gets worse, even if the total amount of happiness in each life is the same. If they are right, such lives have value *as wholes*, and are value atoms. (If Moore's account of punishment was correct, then wholes consisting of wrongdoing and punishment are value atoms too—not value atoms of well-being, but of intrinsic value *simpliciter*.) On the other hand, something's value *on the whole* is its overall value, taking into account both its value *as a whole* and the values of its parts taken individually. In the case of punishment, even though the wrongdoing and punishment together have value as a whole in virtue of the fit between the parts, when the

[70] For more on value as a whole and value on the whole, see sect. 128–9 of Moore 1903.

badness of the component parts are added in, the whole is bad on the whole. Conversely, someone's life may have value on the whole without having value as a whole. For example, consider a life that has lots of good moments, but whose parts do not fit together nicely—for example, it does not get better as it goes along. Such a life could be good on the whole despite not telling a particularly good story.

I hypothesize that Velleman may have had in mind value *as* a whole, rather than value on the whole, when discussing CCC. Thus we may state a revised version of CCC as follows:

> CCC′: Nothing can have intrinsic value *as a whole* for an individual unless that individual has the capacity to care about it as a whole.

I take no stand here on whether CCC′ is true, but it seems more plausible than Velleman's version of the principle. If, as Velleman says, 'a cow has no interest in its life as a whole,' its life lacks value as a whole; but its life may still have value *on the whole*, in virtue of the values of its moments. Thus, CCC′ is compatible with the badness of cows' deaths. It is also compatible with the intuitively obvious claim that a future without torture is better for a cow than one with torture. Cows can care about the moments that make up their lives, even if they cannot care about their lives as a whole. That is enough for their lives to be good or bad for them.

In fact, CCC′ fits better with some of the things Velleman says. In arguing for the claim that extended periods of time have no value for a cow, he says the following:

This point follows most clearly from desire-based conceptions of well-being, which will define how valuable different sequences of harms and benefits are for a cow in terms of how much the cow wants those sequences, or would want them under some ideal conditions. Since a cow cannot care about sequences of harms and benefits, and would not be able to care about them except under conditions that transformed it into something other than a cow, these definitions imply that temporal sequences cannot be assigned a value specifically for a cow.[71]

Note first that Velleman formulates desire satisfactionism in the objectualist way (see Section 1.3)—what is intrinsically valuable for

---

[71] Velleman 1993, 401 n. 45.

someone is that the objects of her desires obtain, rather than the combination of the desires and their objects. Velleman says that according to the desire satisfactionist, how good or bad a sequence is for someone depends on how much the individual wants it. But we must be careful about what sort of value we are talking about here. To take a simple example, suppose Susan desires today, to degree n, that she hugs her dog; suppose tomorrow Susan desires, to degree m, that she drinks a beer. Now suppose she hugs her dog today and drinks a beer tomorrow. The desire satisfactionist should say that this result is good for Susan to degree $m + n$. This is so even if, as seems likely, Susan *never explicitly contemplates or desires the conjunction or sequence of events as such*. In fact, Susan need not even have the capacity to do so. That is because in order to determine the value of a complex whole for a person, the desire satisfactionist instructs us, I assume, to add the basic intrinsic values of the desire satisfactions and frustrations it contains. So the desire satisfactionist may well deny that how good a sequence is for an individual depends on how much the individual wants that sequence. Thus, the desire satisfactionist should reject CCC, but should accept CCC′. In order for a sequence to be a value atom for an individual, that person must desire it, according to objectualism; and you cannot desire something without being able to conceive it; so a sequence cannot be a value atom for a cow. But this is compatible with the sequence having *non-basic* intrinsic value for the cow that derives from the basic intrinsic values of the value atoms in the sequence. And that is all that is needed to get the conclusion that death is bad for the cow.

It seems, then, that just as in the case of babies and fetuses, there is no good reason to discount the badness of death for an animal. If an animal would have had a good life, then killing it is bad for it, even if it cannot contemplate its future. In closing this chapter, I should emphasize that even though death is bad for fetuses, babies, and non-human animals, it does not follow that abortion is morally wrong, or that vegetarianism is morally obligatory. I think, but will not argue here, that there are important differences between the cases of abortion and meat-eating; there are other factors (e.g. the strong interests of the mother) that are weighty enough to make at least some abortions morally permissible, but in most instances there are no similarly weighty interests that could make carnivorism justified. To justify such claims would take many pages. For now, I note simply that while there might be other justifications one might give for eating hamburgers, it cannot be argued that turning cows into hamburgers is not bad for the cows.

5

CAN DEATH BE DEFEATED?

Once I lived like the gods, and more is not needed.

Friedrich Hölderlin[1]

SINCE we are all going to die, we might think it would be worthwhile to find a way to diminish or eliminate death's badness. Roy Sorensen describes an ingenious way to do this: compress an infinite life into a finite period of time.

An infinite amount of personal time can be squeezed into two minutes of external time. During the first minute, the pseudo-immortal lives the first day of his life. During the next half minute, the pseudo-immortal lives the second day. During the following quarter minute, a third day passes. Since there are infinitely many junctures in this sequence, the pseudo-immortal will enjoy infinitely many personal days ... Death will have lost its sting.[2]

To the pseudo-immortal, life seems to last forever, but from an external perspective, his life appears to be on fast-forward, getting faster and faster as it goes, lasting only two minutes. Since you would not be able to tell the difference between an immortal and a pseudo-immortal life from the inside, it would be hard to care much about which one you had, even though pseudo-immortals die and immortals do not. If we could become pseudo-immortals, I think we would succeed in defeating the badness of death.

---

[1] 'To the Fates,' as quoted in McMahan 2002, 137.   [2] Sorensen 2005, 122.

Unfortunately, it is not much easier to become a pseudo-immortal than to become a genuine immortal. Either way, magic would be involved. Is there any non-magical way to make your death less bad for you?

Here are two other ways that work. First: *live for a really long time.* If you do this, by the time you die, your death will not deprive you of very much, because even if you had not died when you did, you would not have lived much longer anyway. This is a practical strategy, and I recommend it highly. But it requires patience! If you are not patient, and you want to make sure your death is not very bad for you, you could be like Chuck. Chuck has hired a pair of assassins to kill him. Assassin 1 plans to kill Chuck at noon tomorrow by dropping a 10-ton block of cheese on him. Assassin 2 plans to kill Chuck tomorrow at 12:05 by shooting him. These assassins never fail. Thus, when Chuck is killed by the cheese, his death will not be very bad for him, since his death will deprive him of only five minutes of life. Like the very old person, Chuck has defeated the badness of death, but at great cost! I do not recommend Chuck's strategy.

The strategies just considered involve an attempt to make death less bad by ensuring that there is no valuable future for it to take away. But not having a valuable future seems like an undesirable situation to be in. Is there a way to have a valuable future ahead of you at the time of your death and still have your death be not very bad for you? Some have thought that it is possible to defeat death by living a really great life, and especially by achieving great things. Call this the *Hölderlin strategy*. On a strong version of the Hölderlin strategy, it is possible to achieve so much early in your life that if you lived any longer, you'd only make your life worse. Even if living longer would be enjoyable for you, 'more is not needed'—and in fact should be avoided. Thus, death would actually be good for you. On a weaker version of the Hölderlin strategy, living a really good life does not make your death good for you. But it does make your death *less bad* for you than it would have been if your life had not been so great before. In this chapter I will examine the plausibility of both versions of the Hölderlin strategy.

5.1 The James Dean Effect

In a very interesting recent study, psychologists Ed Diener, Derrick Wirtz, and Shigehiro Oishi have documented what they call the 'James Dean Effect.'[3] Consider the following way things could have gone for James Dean. Instead of dying in a car accident at age 24, he survives several more years. During those years he stars in *Giant 2: Electric Boogaloo*, then quits the movie business to make a living as an Elvis-style nightclub entertainer. He is happy and (to a degree) successful during that period of time, but not as happy or successful as he was in young adulthood. Would this have been a better life for him than his actual, shorter life? Evidently, people are consistently inclined to say it would not have been better; in Figure 5.1, people typically say that the shorter life is better on the whole.

Diener, Wirtz, and Oishi also note what they call the 'Alexander Solzhenitsyn Effect'. Solzhenitsyn seems not to have been very happy even after his release from prison, but was presumably somewhat less

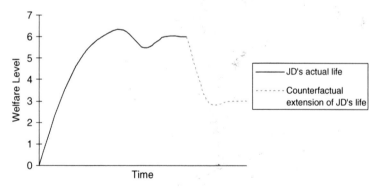

Figure 5.1 (The James Dean Effect)

[3] Diener, Wirtz, and Oishi 2001, 127. The authors note that when asked to choose for themselves, people only *slightly* prefer James Dean's life to a longer one with a mild period at the end, but *strongly* prefer the longer Solzhenitsyn life (127).

unhappy. Would a shorter life have been better for him? If someone lives a miserable life for a long time, people consistently judge it to be better to add an extra period of relatively mild unhappiness to the end, even if that period of unhappiness is not worth having in itself. This is illustrated in Figure 5.2, where people are inclined to say that the longer life is better on the whole.

The judgments described by Diener, Wirtz, and Oishi echo those made by philosophers such as Velleman, who writes:

A person may rationally be willing to die even though he can look forward to a few more good weeks or months; and a person may rationally be unwilling to die even though he can look forward only to continued adversity. The rationality of the patient's attitude depends on whether an earlier or later death would make a better ending to his life story.[4]

In the cases of Dean and Solzhenitsyn, their actual life stories seem to most people to be better (in certain ways at least) than the imagined alternative life stories.

We can now see a way to argue for the strong Hölderlin strategy. If additional years of good life could fail to improve the value of a person's life, or if additional years of bad life could fail to make it worse overall, then lives are *organic unities*—their values are not

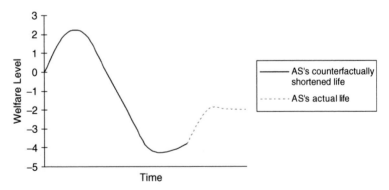

Figure 5.2 (The Alexander Solzhenitsyn Effect)

[4] Velleman 1993, 347. See Strawson 2004 for a critique of the 'life story' view.

determined by summing the values of their parts.[5] Now, suppose that the Difference-Making Principle (DMP) is true. If Dean's life would not have been better with the extra ten mildly good years, and if DMP is true, then Dean's death was not bad for him—in fact, supposing that the extra years of mildly good life would have made his life *worse* overall (as people seem to think), his death was good for him! Perhaps this is a way to defeat death: go out on top, when you have nowhere to go but down.

But this cannot possibly be right, can it? Surely James Dean's death was bad for him. So the following three propositions form an inconsistent triad:

1. James Dean's actual life is better than the life he would have had if he had not died when he did.
2. James Dean's death was bad for him.
3. DMP is true.

To be consistent, we must reject one of these propositions. Suppose we were to reject DMP. How could (1) and (2) both be true? Perhaps what is relevant to the badness of someone's death is not its impact on the person's life *on the whole*, but its impact on the person's *future*. Call this view the ***Future Difference-Making Principle***, or Future-DMP:

Future-DMP: The overall value of an event, occurring at time t, for an individual = how well-off she is *throughout the rest of her life starting at t*, minus how well-off she would have been *throughout the rest of her life starting at t* if the event had not occurred.

If Future-DMP were true, then Dean's death could have been bad for him even if his future goods would not have improved the value of his life on the whole. They would have improved the value of his future, which according to Future-DMP is all that matters in the evaluation of his death.

I have no objection to Future-DMP, since if pure hedonism is true, DMP and Future-DMP are necessarily equivalent. However,

---

[5] The notion of organic unity in axiology was popularized by G. E. Moore (1903).

I do have an objection to the conjunction of Future-DMP and the popular claim that James Dean's life would not have been better if it had lasted longer. Suppose you are presented with the baby James Dean, and told, by an omniscient and omnipotent deity, to determine the future course of his life. You have two choices. In L1, his life goes just as it does in the actual world. In L2, it goes just that way except that an extra ten mildly good years are added on to the end. If you agree with many people's opinions about those two lives, you will think the better future is the one where he dies earlier. *Taken as a whole*, that future is better (even though the total sum of goodness is less). So Future-DMP entails that it would be good for Dean if you chose the shorter future. Now suppose it is just before Dean's death is to occur. The deity returns and allows you to change your mind. Dean is now faced with a future of ten mildly good years or no future at all. It seems it would be better for Dean if you changed your mind, since the mildly good years would be a better future than no future. Future-DMP entails that it would be good for Dean if you now chose the longer future. But how can that be? There does not seem to be any good reason to change your mind in this case. You knew, at the start, how his life was going to go; nothing unexpected has happened. All that has happened is that some time has passed, and Dean has lived some of his life. The result of your choice is the same no matter when it is made.[6]

I cannot think of a plausible replacement for DMP that reconciles (1) and (2). We must reject one of those propositions. Given this choice, I think it is clear that (1) must go. I find it strange that so many people are apparently willing to say that Dean's life would not have been better overall with an extra ten good years added on to the end of it. It appears that people are systematically irrational in their judgments in this area. Perhaps we tend to be misled by our aesthetic intuitions; Dean's actual life makes for a better story than the imagined longer life, but this clearly has nothing to do with whether it is a better life *for him*. The idea that lives are organic

---

[6] For a similar argument in a different context, see Huemer 2003, 160–1.

unities has much more plausibility concerning aesthetic judgments than concerning judgments about well-being. I do not know whether this is the source of the error, but that people make an error seems clear. Of course, some people may desire to live a life that makes for a good story, and given an appropriate theory of well-being, living such a life might be better for such people. But as Galen Strawson has pointed out, not everyone cares about such things, and it is not clear why they should if they do not.[7]

So the strong Hölderlin strategy is not plausible; it is more plausible to deny that James Dean lived a better life than he would have if he'd lived than it is to claim that his death was good for him, or to deny DMP. This result has repercussions. It should lead us to question narrative structure views of well-being, since it is such views that lead us to the unpalatable result about James Dean's life.

Defenders of narrative structure views ('narrativists') may well be unmoved. One reply available to the narrativist who wishes to claim that James Dean's death was good for him is to argue that it is sometimes not best to choose the best future. For example, when one has worked towards certain goals in the past, and one must choose between achieving those goals and having a worse future or not achieving them and having a better future, might it not be perfectly rational to choose to achieve the goals? Would it not make one's life as a whole go better? The narrativist might appeal to Socrates here, and point out that he thought his decision to take the hemlock rather than survive in exile was rational. Socrates evidently would have seen the decision to continue living as a betrayal of what he lived for. If it can make sense to choose the worse future, then the value of a life must be determined partly by global features such as narrative structure.

But the most plausible of these cases are cases where the person does not want the allegedly good future, but prefers to die instead, like Socrates. When a sane, informed person prefers death to continued life, there is an inclination to think continued survival would not

<hr/>

[7] Strawson 2004.

result in a good future for that person. A desire satisfactionist, for example, might conclude from the fact that Socrates preferred to die that the future where he dies is a better future for him than the one where he lives. If so, this is not a case in which someone rationally chooses the worse future after all. In order to be sure that we are testing the appropriate intuition, the narrativist needs a case where the person prefers to live, and her future would be good for her, but the person's death still seems to be good for her. I cannot think of any plausible case like this. In cases in which the person does *not* prefer to die, and correctly thinks her future would be good for her, it is bizarre to say that her death is good for her, or that she is making a mistake in wanting to continue living.

Another move for the narrativist would be to agree that James Dean's death was bad, and that his life would indeed have been better had he lived the ten extra years, but that due to the downward trajectory his life would have taken, his good future would not have made as much of a difference to his life as it would have to, say, Alexander Solzhenitsyn's life. The contribution that a period of goodness makes to the value of a life on the whole is *enhanced* or *discounted* by its contribution to the person's narrative, but it is never *transvalued*: that is, a good period of life never makes a negative contribution to lifetime value, and a bad period never makes a positive contribution. This more modest view supports the weak Hölderlin strategy, since it entails that the badness of death need not be proportional to the goodness of the future it takes away.

This more modest view seems more plausible. However, we have little reason to accept it. The modest view is supported by an appeal to intuitions about the values of lives that get better or worse at the end. And if I'm right that (2) is more plausible than (1), and that they are inconsistent, we must conclude that people's intuitions about the values of lives that improve or decline at the end are unreliable. People systematically overrate the value of a life that improves at the end, and underrate the value of a life that declines at the end. This gives us reason to doubt the evidence adduced in favor of even modest narrative structure views, and therefore provides more support for the pure hedonism I defended in Chapter I.

So we must look elsewhere for a defense of the Hölderlin strategy. I turn now to a defense of the weak Hölderlin strategy that does not depend on an appeal to a narrative structure view about well-being. The basic idea is suggested by things we sometimes say about the recently deceased, such as 'at least she lived a full life.'[8] Kai Draper notes that 'so long as one does well with respect to a given sort of good ... not doing as well as one was likely to have done with respect to that good is typically not *terribly* disappointing.'[9] It is not just in cases of death in old age that we feel this way; we may have a similar intuition in the case of a young novelist who completes his great novel just before his death.[10] By completing his novel, the young novelist makes his life better, thereby lessening the evil of his death. Walter Kaufmann expresses something like this idea in the following passage:

Not only in childhood but long after one may retain the feeling that one is ... at the mercy of death. 'But once what I am bent on, what is holy, my poetry, is accomplished,' once I have succeeded in achieving—in the face of death, in a race with death—a project that is truly mine, ... then the picture changes: I have won the race and in a sense have triumphed over death. Death and madness come too late.[11]

I've already argued in Chapter I that achievement is not intrinsically good. But suppose my arguments fail; has Kaufmann described a defensible version of the weak Hölderlin strategy? If so, I suppose that might be a good thing for us. But it would be bad news for DMP. DMP entails that the extent to which death is bad is determined entirely by the relation between the value of the life a person lives and the value of the life she would have lived had she not died; the value of what came before is irrelevant.

---

[8] I assume that by a 'full life' we typically mean a life that had lots of goods in it, or perhaps many different sorts of goods, rather than, say, a life that had no more room for any more goods. It is possible that people mean something else when they say a life is 'full,' but I do not know what it is.

[9] Draper 1999, 397.   [10] See McMahan 2002, 140.

[11] Kaufmann 1961, 382; quoted in McMahan 2002, 138.

5.2 Old Age and Progeria

Here are two examples that McMahan suggests pose a problem for DMP:

> *The Geriatric Patient:* A woman reaches the maximum life span, the biological limits of human life. Every organ is on the verge of failing when she dies suddenly of a massive hemorrhagic stroke.[12]
>
> *The Progeria Patient:* A child of twelve dies from progeria in a state of advanced decrepitude.[13] (Progeria is a rare disease that causes something like premature aging.)

The examples of the Progeria Patient and the Geriatric Patient are intended to be similar in certain relevant ways, so let us add to the description of the Progeria Patient that like the Geriatric Patient, he dies of a hemorrhagic stroke just before organ failure would have occurred. Let us also add this important detail: the Geriatric Patient's life contained a great many goods, while the Progeria Patient's life contained far fewer.

McMahan thinks DMP has difficulties accounting for the misfortunes of the Geriatric Patient and the Progeria Patient. According to McMahan, both suffer misfortunes, but the Progeria Patient's misfortune is much greater. If we stipulate that the Geriatric Patient and the Progeria Patient are deprived of the same amount of goods in death, DMP entails that their deaths are equally unfortunate.

But is it really such a great misfortune for the Progeria Patient to die? The Progeria Patient is stipulated to be in a decrepit condition. Given that he is in such a state, with so little to look forward to, it seems wrong to say that *death itself* is a great misfortune for the Progeria Patient. But of course, the Progeria Patient does suffer a great misfortune of another sort. McMahan makes a distinction between the misfortune of death itself and two other sorts of misfortune. There are the *overall misfortunes in dying*, including those misfortunes attributable not to death itself, but to events or states associated with death in some way. There is also the misfortune of *having no more*

---

[12] McMahan 2002, 117.   [13] McMahan 2002, 134.

goods in prospect whether one dies or not.[14] This last sort of misfortune is suffered by the Geriatric Patient and the Progeria Patient.[15] Even were they to survive a bit longer, they would not be getting much out of their lives given their decrepitude. The problem for DMP is that it entails that the Geriatric Patient and the Progeria Patient suffer misfortunes of precisely the same magnitude, given what their life prospects would have been had they not died when they did. But the Progeria Patient's situation seems much more unfortunate than the Geriatric Patient's.

At this point we should notice that if it is right to say that the misfortunes suffered by the Geriatric Patient and the Progeria Patient are not properly attributed to their deaths, then the examples pose no problems for DMP *as a view about the value of death itself*. However, since DMP is a general account of overall badness, it must also account for the other misfortunes associated with death. The problem is that DMP seems incompatible with the view that the Progeria Patient's misfortune is greater than the Geriatric Patient's. After all, for any misfortune the Progeria Patient suffers, there seems to be an analogous one suffered by the Geriatric Patient. Dying deprives neither of much; neither has much to look forward to. McMahan has a hypothesis about why the Progeria Patient's misfortune seems greater: 'The reason that it seems a greater misfortune for the Progeria Patient to have arrived at a point at which no further good is possible is that he has gained so little—and so much less—from life. The Geriatric Patient has already had a full life; the Progeria Patient has not.'[16] McMahan here asserts a connection between the evil of death and the value of the life that preceded it: other things equal (such as the value of the future death takes away), the better someone's life went, the less bad his death is. If this is right, then DMP is false, and the weak Hölderlin strategy is vindicated.

Is McMahan right about this? Some of the sorts of things we say at funerals—e.g., 'at least she lived a full life'—seem to provide some evidence for McMahan's claim. But we should not take this too seriously. There are many things we might be trying to express when

---

[14] McMahan 2002, 127 and 134–5.   [15] McMahan 2002, 135.
[16] McMahan 2002, 135.

we say that someone has lived a full life. We might simply be saying, in accord with DMP, that her death was less bad than it would have been had she died earlier and therefore been deprived of more of a good life. Similarly, we might be saying that her death is less bad than many other people's deaths, since many people die in childhood or early adulthood. Or we may be just changing the subject, in order to console others or ourselves. We may not be trying to suggest that death is not so bad, but rather to take our minds off the evil of death by thinking about something intrinsically good, such as the life of the recently deceased. This is a very common phenomenon. When someone loses his job and is divorced by his wife, we might cheer him up by saying 'at least you have your health.' This does not help to show that the person's misfortunes are less bad than he thought. It just reminds the person that despite the great misfortunes he has suffered, there is another misfortune that he has managed to avoid. Perhaps the same thing is happening when we console the relatives of the recently deceased by reminding them that she lived a good life.[17]

These remarks may seem tendentious; in any case, we cannot settle the issue of the relation between the evil of death and the life that preceded it just by examining the things we say at funerals. The real problem with McMahan's hypothesis is that it is hard to see how to construct a plausible view according to which the value of a person's life necessarily affects the value of his death.

5.3 Previous Gains and Discounts

The simplest view according to which the value of a death is determined by the value of the life that preceded it is what McMahan calls the *Previous Gain Account*. According to this view, 'the badness of a death is inversely proportional to the extent to which the life it ends was good overall.'[18] But the Previous Gain Account is too simplistic. McMahan rejects the Previous Gain Account because it goes wrong

[17] Thanks to Ned Markosian for discussion of this response. I believe he first suggested the 'changing the subject' reply to me.

[18] McMahan 2002, 136.

in the case of Mozart's death.[19] Mozart accomplished a great deal in a very short life. Accomplishment is, according to McMahan, one important part of personal well-being. So the Previous Gain Account seems committed to the view that Mozart's death was one of the least bad deaths anyone ever died. But of course, most of us consider his death very tragic. Had he not died, he had a lot of great life ahead of him. The Previous Gain Account completely ignores what Mozart lost out on by dying young, and looks *only* at what he did while he was alive.

In light of the example of Mozart, McMahan's solution is to *discount* the misfortune of death for previous gains in life.[20] (This is in addition to the discount applied for lack of psychological connection, as discussed in Section 4.4.) The discounting view does not entail that Mozart's death is not very bad. What Mozart lost out on in dying plays *some* role in determining how bad his death is, but the fact that he accomplished so much *mitigates* the badness of his death.

At this point we need to be more precise about what it means to 'discount' the misfortune suffered in dying. McMahan suggests we *multiply* the value of the misfortune by a fraction depending on the value of the life.[21] For example, someone who lives a very fortunate life might get a 20 percent discount on the badness of her death (the value of the misfortune of her death would be multiplied by $4/5$), while someone who lives an unfortunate life might get no discount. Call this the 'Percentage Discount View.' We might formulate the view more precisely as follows:

The Percentage Discount View (PDV): The value of event E for person S at world w = (the intrinsic value of w for S, minus the intrinsic value for S of the closest world to w where E does not occur) multiplied by some n ($0 < n < 1$) corresponding to the value of S's actual life. As S's life gets better, n gets smaller.

PDV gets the result McMahan wants in the case of the young novelist. His death deprives him of some goods, but the misfortune of that

---

[19] McMahan 2002, 140.   [20] McMahan 2002, 144.
[21] Personal correspondence. Another possible view would have us *add* or *subtract* some value based on previous fortune or misfortune, rather than multiply. My criticisms of PDV would apply to this view as well.

deprivation is discounted by some percentage due to the fact that he completed a novel. But when we try to explain why the Progeria Patient's situation is more tragic than the Geriatric Patient's, we run into trouble. According to McMahan, the Progeria Patient's *death* is no worse for him than the Geriatric Patient's is for her. It is the other related misfortune, the absence of future goods to which to look forward, that gets discounted more in the Geriatric Patient's case than in the Progeria Patient's.

The Progeria Patient and the Geriatric Patient have virtually no losses at all, but this is because the conditions of their lives preclude the possibility of further good, and this itself may be a misfortune. I suggest that all three types of misfortune can plausibly be discounted for the magnitude of the victim's previous gains from life.[22]

We should discount the misfortune a person suffers in dying (whether the misfortune is the loss caused by death, the overall loss, or simply the arrival at a point at which no further good is possible) for the magnitude of the person's previous gains from life.[23]

So it is not just the misfortune of death itself that gets discounted for previous gains in life. But this raises a question for discounting views in general: Which misfortunes are subject to discount? It seems implausible to suppose that *all* misfortunes are discounted. If I stub my toe, it hurts just as much if I've had a good life as if I have not, and the pain does not seem to be any less bad for me. Having been well-off in the past does not give me a magic shield against misfortunes generally. But it is difficult to find a non-arbitrary criterion to distinguish the misfortunes that are discounted from the ones that are not.

McMahan claims that it is only *misfortunes of deprivation* that are discounted, because they are 'essentially comparative.'[24] But

---

[22] McMahan 2002, 141.   [23] McMahan 2002, 144.

[24] Personal correspondence. McMahan also suggests, again in personal correspondence, that the misfortune of having no future goods to look forward to cannot be discounted in the way described by PDV, since that misfortune cannot be assigned a numerical value. This suggests a departure from the position he takes in the passages quoted above, since he clearly wants to discount the badness of the Geriatric Patient's death. Furthermore, I think there is no good reason to

misfortunes of deprivation cannot be neatly separated from other misfortunes; sometimes an event will cause some good or bad things, while also preventing others. Such cases pose serious problems for McMahan's proposal. Suppose that if event E were to occur, it would cause states of affairs with value +9 for subject S, but would also prevent states of affairs with value +10 for S. Thus it is both a prima facie non-deprivational fortune and a prima facie deprivational misfortune. Would E be good for S or not? If McMahan is right, the value for S of the non-deprivational fortune involved in receiving goods with value +9 is not subject to discount no matter how well things have gone for S in the past. It is not an essentially comparative fortune. But the value for S of the deprivational misfortune involved in being deprived of goods with value +10 is an essentially comparative misfortune, so it is subject to discount. Thus, whether E is good overall for S depends on how well things have gone for S in the past. If S has had a poor life so far, the misfortune of being deprived of goods with value of +10 is not discounted; thus, E would be bad for S overall (9 minus 10 equals −1). If S has had a very fortunate life so far, that misfortune is discounted; if the discount is, say, 20 percent, E turns out to be good for S overall (9 minus (10 × .8) equals +1). This is an unacceptable result. Whether E is a good deal for S or not does not depend on how well S's life has gone.

Thus, it seems better to say that *all* misfortunes are essentially comparative; a misfortune is a misfortune because it makes its victim worse off than he would have been otherwise. This is what DMP says. Different misfortunes do this in different ways. Some make the victim worse off by causing something intrinsically bad to happen to him; others by preventing something good from happening to him; and still others by doing both.

One might think that there are some misfortunes, such as pain, that are not essentially comparative, but rather 'just plain bad.' But here it is important to make a distinction between overall misfortunes and

---

say that no numerical value can be assigned to such misfortunes, as long as there is a numerical value for the intrinsic goods the person would have received if he had not reached a point of having none in store. Perhaps there is a problem with assigning these numerical values, but it is no more of a problem than in the case of having nothing to look forward to.

intrinsic misfortunes. We might say that pain is always *intrinsically* bad, and that whether an episode of pain is an intrinsic misfortune for someone does not involve any comparisons with other ways the person's life might have gone. But an actual episode of pain is not an *overall* misfortune merely in virtue of the way things actually go. Whether it is an overall misfortune depends also on whether, for example, it prevents another, worse pain; thus, whether it is an overall misfortune depends on relations between an actual life and a counterfactual one. This distinction between types of misfortunes cannot provide the distinction between discounted and non-discounted misfortunes that McMahan is after; what McMahan needs is a non-arbitrary way to distinguish the *overall* misfortunes that are discounted from those that are not. I see no way to make that distinction.

5.4 Realism

Suppose, then, that the misfortunes of the Progeria Patient and the Geriatric Patient are not evaluated by appeal to the quality of life each enjoyed before dying. What should we say about their misfortunes, and how do we account for the sense that the Progeria Patient suffers a greater misfortune? McMahan is right to say that their *deaths* are equally unfortunate.[25] What is the misfortune that the Progeria Patient suffers that the Geriatric Patient does not? An obvious answer is that unlike the Geriatric Patient, the Progeria Patient had progeria. Had the Progeria Patient not had progeria, he would presumably have lived a long, relatively happy life. Having progeria deprived the Progeria Patient of lots of goods. DMP has no difficulty in accounting for the great misfortune the Progeria Patient suffers. Of course, DMP also seems to entail that the Geriatric Patient suffers a

---

[25] By the end of the chapter, the reader might wonder whether I really think this sentence is true. I do think it is true, but I also think there are contexts in which it is true to say that the Progeria Patient's death is worse, because a different similarity relation is presupposed. I hope the ensuing discussion makes this clear.

great misfortune: the misfortune of being an ordinary human being subject to the aging process. Had the Geriatric Patient not been subject to the ordinary rigors of aging, she would have lived a lot longer and presumably happier life. What, then, is the difference between the two?

There is a principle that McMahan calls the 'Realism Condition' that could help explain what is going on here, but perhaps not in just the way McMahan has in mind. The Realism Condition is the following principle about losses: 'for there to be a loss, a good must have been genuinely in prospect but then have been prevented by some intervening condition.'[26] Kai Draper makes use of a similar principle in attempting to distinguish genuine evils from mere comparative evils that are unworthy of disappointment (as discussed in Section 2.3): 'Whenever someone is prevented from receiving a large benefit that she was very likely to receive and, hence, reasonably hoped to receive, she has suffered a misfortune.'[27] It is considerably more realistic or reasonable to suppose that the Progeria Patient had some goods in store that were taken away by his progeria than to suppose that the Geriatric Patient had some goods in store that were taken away by the fact that she was subject to the rigors of aging. The nearest possible world where the Progeria Patient lives a long and healthy life is not much different from the actual world, while different biological laws must govern the nearest world where the Geriatric Patient remains alive and healthy to age 185.

In suggesting that we make use of the Realism Condition (or, alternatively, Draper's 'likelihood' constraint), I am not suggesting that we take it as a serious piece of ethical theory, to be built into our account of misfortune, but rather as a pragmatic constraint governing the choice of similarity relation, and hence which counterfactual lives may appropriately be considered as a term of comparison in DMP. When we insist on realism, we rule out similarity relations that count worlds with very different laws of nature as similar to the actual world. So DMP does enable us to say, at least in contexts in which realism is important, that the Progeria Patient's overall losses are greater than

---

[26] McMahan 2002, 133.   [27] Draper 1999, 393.

the Geriatric Patient's.[28] Of course, the Realism Condition may be ignored in certain contexts, such as contexts where we are seriously considering unrealistic possibilities such as extremely long life or immortality.[29] In such contexts, the actual length of human life does seem like a misfortune for all humans.

DMP does not *require* us to say that the Progeria Patient's losses are greater than the Geriatric Patient's. Some might be concerned about the fact that different similarity relations yield different value judgments. Here are some events that could have happened had the Progeria Patient's actual death at t_p not occurred:

E1: the Progeria Patient dies from the hemorrhage at some time after t_p.

E2: the Progeria Patient dies at t_p, but not from the hemorrhage.

E3: the Progeria Patient's progeria is cured.

E4: the Progeria Patient is born without progeria.

I think it is often implicitly supposed that there is one universally correct answer, that applies in every context, to the question of which event would have happened had the Progeria Patient's actual death not occurred. But this is not the case. The particular line of inquiry in which we are engaged will determine a similarity relation; different inquiries make salient different similarity relations, which in turn yield different answers to the question of what would have happened.

This may seem problematic. While there will be choices of similarity relation that will result in the Progeria Patient's death being worse than the Geriatric Patient's, there will also be choices that

---

[28] Feit suggests a way to reformulate a comparative view to account for Draper's intuitions, involving restricting accessibility relations between worlds (Feit 2002, 376). There might not be much difference between my view and Feit's on this issue.

[29] McMahan claims that a comparison between death and immortality is 'the wrong comparison; it is not what we are most interested in' (McMahan 2002, 104). But what we are interested in changes depending on conversational context, and clearly there are some contexts in which people are interested in this comparison, as evidenced by Bernard Williams's much-discussed 'Makropulos Case' (Williams 1993).

will yield the opposite result.[30] But surely that cannot be right; is it not *unequivocally true* that the Progeria Patient's misfortune is greater?

This much is true: a very short life like the Progeria Patient's contains less intrinsic value, less well-being, than a long, full, happy life like the Geriatric Patient's. But when it comes to determinations of *overall values* of particular events in people's lives, we must simply abandon the idea that there are always unequivocal, context-invariant answers to the question of whose misfortune is greater. Given DMP, the question of whether the Progeria Patient's death is worse than the Geriatric Patient's must be regarded as incomplete. We get an answer to the question of whether the Progeria Patient's misfortune is worse than the Geriatric Patient's only given a similarity relation. John Broome claims that 'all the significant facts have been fully stated once we have said what dying at eighty-two is better than and what it is worse than. There is no further significant question whether or not dying at eighty-two is an absolutely bad thing.'[31] The point as I see it is that, once we have determined the value of a death relative to a similarity relation, we do not go on to determine the *absolute* value of E. Value relative to a similarity relation is all there is, at least when it comes to overall value.

In insisting on adding realism and reasonableness constraints to the evaluations of deaths, McMahan and Draper add unnecessary complications to their views. They also make it difficult to make sense of certain apparently true evaluations of deaths made in unusual contexts in which unrealistic possibilities are being seriously considered. What they are really after is restrictions on the similarity relation. But the attempt to give general restrictions of this sort is hopeless.

---

[30] Thanks to Peter Menzies for discussion of this point.

[31] Broome 1999, 171. Broome's overarching concern is to eliminate the notion of 'absolute' goodness in favor of a comparative notion of betterness, whereas I am concerned to eliminate talk of absolute goodness only when *extrinsic* goodness or badness is at issue. The view endorsed here is entirely compatible with the existence of absolute intrinsic goodness. The extent to which something is intrinsically good does not depend on any comparisons. Rather, as Moore claimed (1922, 260) and I argued in Section 1.3, something's intrinsic value depends solely on its intrinsic nature.

The restrictions are provided by rules of conversation, which are vague, flexible, and defeasible. It is a bad idea to try to precisify such rules as part of the attempt to provide fundamental principles about value.

Another complication is worth considering. In the discussion of the Realism Condition above, I claimed that the nearest possible world in which the Progeria Patient does not have progeria need not be an unrealistic world with different laws of nature. This presupposes that *there is* a possible world in which the Progeria Patient does not have progeria. This might be questioned. It is sometimes thought that a person's origins are essential to him.[32] If so, then given some further assumptions about the essences of gametes, it could turn out that a person's genetic makeup is essential to him. Call this view 'genetic essentialism.' Progeria is a genetic disease; according to the Progeria Research Foundation, the likely cause is a single mutant gene.[33] If we are to use DMP to determine how bad it is for the Progeria Patient that he was born with progeria rather than being born without it, we need to suppose that there is a possible world at which he is born without progeria. But given genetic essentialism, there is no possible world in which the Progeria Patient exists but was not born with progeria.[34] Thus DMP prevents us from saying that it is bad for the Progeria Patient that he was born with progeria rather than not.[35]

We might avoid this problem by rejecting genetic essentialism. It certainly seems possible to imagine a particular person having existed with a different set of genes, which provides at least prima facie evidence against the essentiality claim. The genetic essentialist might say that what we are really imagining is not that very person existing with different genes, but a different person with some of the same

[32] See Kripke's famous discussion of Queen Elizabeth (Kripke 1972, 113).

[33] <http://www.progeriaresearch.org/about_progeria.html>.

[34] This assumes that possession of the gene invariably results in having progeria. If this assumption is false, then so much the worse for the objection, and so much the better for DMP.

[35] Thanks to Tim Bayne and Ernest Sosa for discussion of this objection.

characteristics. But it is hard to see the motivation for such a claim. Even if we grant that genetic make-up is relevant to cross-world identifications of individuals, we need not and should not require *complete* genetic similarity for cross-world identity. And even if it were essential to the Progeria Patient that he was born with the set of genes he was born with, it would not follow that it is essential to him that his condition is incurable or untreatable.

But this response does not really get to the heart of the problem. Suppose complete genetic similarity is not required for cross-world identity; there could still be *some* genes the possession of which is essential to their owners. We could imagine a different, fictional disease, call it progeria*, that is caused by a set of genes that really is essential to those who have it.[36] We might even stipulate that progeria* cannot be cured or treated without loss of identity. Suppose the Progeria Patient has progeria*. Then the preceding response does not apply.

Perhaps we could admit the existence of *impossible* worlds, and reformulate DMP to allow a comparison between the value of a person's actual life and the value of his life at some nearby impossible world. As long as there is an impossible world in which the Progeria Patient does not have progeria* (and there is), DMP could yield the result that the Progeria Patient's progeria is bad for him even if genetic essentialism is true. The genetic essentialist who refuses to countenance impossible worlds should just admit that the Progeria Patient's having progeria* is not bad for him overall, since having progeria* is a necessary condition for the Progeria Patient's existence at all given genetic essentialism.[37] In the absence of impossible worlds, what is necessarily true cannot be overall bad for anyone.

I conclude that previous gains in life do not affect the evil of death, nor of any other misfortunes. On the bright side, we have found

---

[36] Thanks to Jeff McMahan for this suggestion.

[37] This raises problems of the sort discussed by Parfit in ch. 16 of Parfit 1984. For example, it would entail that causing someone to be born with progeria would not be bad for him, and hence not harm him; after all, had the person not been born with progeria, he would not have existed at all. These are very difficult problems and I cannot do justice to them here.

no reason to abandon the simple account of misfortune I have been defending here. On the not so bright side, it seems that there is no way to defeat death's badness; the Hölderlin strategy has not been vindicated even in its weak form. So one of my final tasks is to deal with this potential source of depression.

CONCLUSION

> What difference, then, is it to me how I pass away, whether by
> drowning or by a fever? For by something of the sort I must
> needs pass away.
>
> Epictetus[1]

HERE is what I've shown. Death is typically bad for its victim,
contrary to what Epicurus seems to have thought. How bad death is
for someone depends on what difference it makes to the value of the
victim's life for her—that is, how much better her life would have
gone for her if she had not died then (Chapter 2). The badness of a
death does not depend, in any direct way, on how well things went
for the victim before she died (Chapter 5), or on the psychological
features of the victim at the time of death (e.g., her ability to conceive
of her future), or on facts about psychological unity (Chapter 4).
Thus death is a very bad thing for fetuses, babies, and cows, contrary
to what many have thought (though, as I have pointed out, it does
not follow that it is just as wrong to kill those beings as it is to kill a
typical adult human being). Death is a *timeful* evil; it is bad for people
(and fetuses, and cows) at certain times after they die, but not others
(Chapter 3).

I've also shown that *correspondence theories* of well-being—including
a great many currently popular theories—should be rejected
(Chapter 1). Thus we can conclude that it is impossible to harm

---

[1] Epictetus, *Arrian's Discourses*, Bk II, ch. 5, 10–14, trans. Oldfather, as quoted
in Kramer and Wu 1988, 120.

someone after she has died. Since correspondence theories should be rejected, we have good reason to consider *pure hedonism* to be a viable theory of well-being.

In the process, I've shown some other things whose importance is perhaps more obscure to those who are not actively researching in axiology, but that should be of some interest to a handful of professional philosophers. For instance, I've shown that something's intrinsic value depends solely on its intrinsic properties (Section 1.3); that (assuming Lewisian semantics for counterfactuals) the overall value of an event is relative to a similarity relation (Section 2.1); and that a dead person has a well-being level of zero (Section 3.5).

Some will think that there is something about death that I've missed. I've argued that bad feelings about death are rational (Section 2.3). I've compared the badness of death to the badness of having one's tickets to a baseball game secretly stolen—the only relevant difference is the magnitude of the badness. But has something not been left out? We feel terror and dread at the prospect of death. We have no such feelings about other deprivations—regret, maybe, but not terror. No matter how many baseball games one missed, one would not feel that sort of terror about it. There is something about the fact that *we'll stop existing altogether* that is terrifying. It is troubling to imagine the world going on without us. (Perhaps it is somewhat less troubling when we realize that people will remember us, that we'll continue to have an impact on the world after we die. But as Roy Sorensen pointed out to me, we are less comforted by this realization when we realize that (i) we have little control over most of that impact—for the most part, our impact is diffuse and seemingly random; and (ii) dogs and tables have a similar impact on the future.) The badness of never existing again just seems fundamentally different from the badness of missing a baseball game—not merely much worse, but different.[2]

I sometimes share these feelings of terror. But I do not see a plausible account of the badness of death that would make sense of them. (This is not to say these feelings about death are irrational—merely

---

[2] Thanks to Kieran Setiya for discussion of this point. For more on this topic, see Part I of Kamm 1993.

that they do not correspond to the actual badness of death, so they would need to be justified in some other way. I doubt any such justification is forthcoming.) For example, one might hold that going out of existence has infinite negative intrinsic value for a person. But the result of this would be that the badness of death utterly swamps all other values, such that the world goes equally badly for everyone who ever lives. That seems pretty implausible. Or one might think there is a completely different *kind* of value that death has, and when something has that kind of value, terror is an appropriate feeling to have towards it. But what is this mysterious other sort of value? It seems most likely that the feelings of terror about death served some evolutionary purpose, and perhaps still serve that purpose sometimes, but we are in general more rational if we overcome or suppress them.

There are other feelings about death that I have not accounted for. Some people care very much about the manner of their deaths. For example, some find it much more disturbing to contemplate being murdered by some evildoer than to die of a disease, or from other 'natural' causes.[3] While I sometimes share these feelings too, I think they have no bearing on the badness of death. Other things being equal, Epictetus was right in this sense: the cause of death does not make any difference at all to how bad the *death* is for its victim. It matters only to how bad the *dying process* is.

Some of the conclusions I've drawn might make people upset. For example, some might be sad to know that it is impossible to make death less bad by writing a great novel or achieving some other noble goal. The most consoling thing I can say is that if your death will be very bad for you, that is actually a really good sign for you.[4] It probably indicates that your life is going well. (This is cold comfort, no doubt.) Of course, it need not be so—things might be going very badly for you, only for you to die just as things would have started going your way.[5] In any case, you do not want to end up in a situation where your death comes as a blessing. And the attempt to make your

---

[3] Kris McDaniel reported this feeling to me.
[4] See Kamm on 'The Good of Senseless Deaths' (1993, 57).
[5] See Nozick 1981, 580 n.

death less bad is misguided anyway.[6] Chuck (Chapter 5) tried to make his death less bad by making it the case that if the cheese had not killed him, the bullet would have killed him shortly afterward. He made his death less bad, but only by making sure that a good life was impossible for him. Bad idea! The best way to make your death less bad is to put it off for as long as a good life is available to you. Sadly, even if you are successful in this endeavor, some great misfortune will befall you—even if it is merely the mundane misfortune of getting old and decrepit.

Some might find the conclusions reached here to be de-motivational. Death will get you in the end, and contrary to what Kaufmann suggests, you will not be able to 'triumph over death' by accomplishing great things, so why bother to do anything at all? The answer is that there are plenty of other reasons to accomplish great things. If you are planning to write a great novel just so you can defeat death, you will be doing it for a bad reason. If you are prudent, you are concerned with the intrinsic value of your life, rather than the extrinsic values of events in your life. Some people would say that just completing the novel is intrinsically good for you. Those people are wrong. But if writing the novel brings you pleasure, it will make things go better for you. That's a good enough reason to do it. So there's your motivation.

There is plenty more to say about death. But in general, a book about death should be either short or funny. And this book definitely does not have enough jokes.

---

[6] McMahan makes a similar point (2002, 129–30), though his aim is not to cheer up the reader.

BIBLIOGRAPHY

ADAMS, ROBERT (1999), *Finite and Infinite Goods* (New York: Oxford University Press).

ANSCOMBE, G. E. M. (1957), *Intention* (Ithaca, NY: Cornell University Press).

ARRHENIUS, GUSTAF (Unpublished), 'The Moral Status of Potential People.' Manuscript, Stockholm University.

BABER, HARRIET (Forthcoming), 'Ex Ante Desire and Post Hoc Satisfaction.' In *Time and Identity*, eds. Campbell, O'Rourke, and Silverstein.

BALASHOV, YURI (1999), 'Zero-Value Physical Quantities.' *Synthese* 119: 253–86.

BAYLIS, CHARLES (1958), 'Grading, Values, and Choice.' *Mind* 67: 485–501.

BELSHAW, CHRIS (2000), 'Later Death/Earlier Birth.' In *Midwest Studies in Philosophy vol. XXIV*, eds. French and Wettstein, 69–83.

—— (2005), *10 Good Questions about Life and Death* (Malden, MA: Blackwell Publishing).

BENATAR, DAVID (ed.) (2004), *Life, Death, & Meaning: Key Philosophical Readings on the Big Questions* (Lanham, MD: Rowman & Littlefield).

—— (2006), *Better Never to Have Been: The Harm of Coming Into Existence* (New York: Oxford University Press).

BIGELOW, JOHN, JOHN CAMPBELL AND ROBERT PARGETTER (1990), 'Death and Well-Being.' *Pacific Philosophical Quarterly* 71: 119–40.

BOGNAR, GERGELY (2004), *Well-Being and Risk*. Doctoral dissertation, Central European University, Budapest, Hungary.

BOONIN, DAVID (2003), *A Defense of Abortion* (New York: Cambridge University Press).

BRADLEY, BEN (1998), 'Extrinsic Value,' *Philosophical Studies* 91: 109–26.

—— (2002), 'Is Intrinsic Value Conditional?' *Philosophical Studies* 107: 23–44.

—— (2004), 'When is Death Bad for the One Who Dies?' *Noûs* 38: 1–28.

—— (2007a), 'How Bad Is Death?' *Canadian Journal of Philosophy* 37: 111–27.

—— (2007b), 'A Paradox for Some Theories of Welfare.' *Philosophical Studies* 133: 45–53.

—— (2008), 'The Worst Time to Die.' *Ethics* 118: 291–314.

—— (Forthcoming), 'Eternalism and Death's Badness.' In *Time and Identity*, eds. Campbell, O'Rourke, and Silverstein.

BRADLEY, BEN AND KRIS McDANIEL (2008), 'Desires.' *Mind* 117: 267–302.

BRANDT, R (1972), 'Rationality, Egoism, and Morality.' *The Journal of Philosophy* 69: 681–97.

BRÄNNMARK, JOHAN (2001), 'Good Lives: Parts and Wholes.' *American Philosophical Quarterly* 38: 221–31.

BROCK, DAN (1992), 'Voluntary Active Euthanasia.' *Hastings Center Report* 22: 10–22.

BROOME, JOHN (1999), *Ethics out of Economics* (Cambridge, U.K.: Cambridge University Press).

—— (2004), *Weighing Lives* (New York: Oxford University Press).

BYKVIST, KRISTER (1998), *Changing Preferences: A Study in Preferentialism.* Doctoral dissertation, Uppsala University.

—— (2007), 'The Benefits of Coming Into Existence.' *Philosophical Studies* 135: 335–62.

CALLAHAN, JOAN (1987), 'On Harming the Dead.' *Ethics* 97: 341–52.

CAMPBELL, JOSEPH, MICHAEL O'ROURKE AND HARRY SILVERSTEIN (eds.) (Forthcoming), *Time and Identity* (Cambridge, MA: MIT Press).

CARLSON, ERIK (1999), 'Consequentialism, Alternatives, and Actualism.' *Philosophical Studies* 96: 253–68.

CARSON, THOMAS (2000), *Value and the Good Life* (Notre Dame, IN: University of Notre Dame Press).

CHANG, RUTH (ed.) (1997), *Incommensurability, Incomparability, and Practical Reason* (Cambridge, MA: Harvard University Press).

CHISHOLM, RODERICK (1976), *Person and Object* (LaSalle, IL: Open Court Publishing Co.).

CONEE, EARL (2006), 'Dispositions toward Counterfactuals in Ethics.' In *The Good, the Right, Life and Death*, eds. McDaniel *et al.*, 173–88.

CRISP, ROGER (2006), *Reasons and the Good* (New York: Oxford University Press).

D'ARMS, JUSTIN AND DANIEL JACOBSON (2000), 'The Moralistic Fallacy: On the "Appropriateness" of Emotions.' *Philosophy and Phenomenological Research* 61: 65–90.

DARWALL, STEPHEN (2002), *Welfare and Rational Care* (Princeton: Princeton University Press).

DeGRAZIA, DAVID (2003), 'Identity, Killing, and the Boundaries of Our Existence.' *Philosophy and Public Affairs* 31: 413–42.

DIENER, ED, DERRICK WIRTZ AND SHIGEHIRO OISHI (2001), 'End Effects of Rated Life Quality: The James Dean Effect.' *Psychological Science* 12: 124–28.

DRAPER, KAI (1999), 'Disappointment, Sadness, and Death.' *The Philosophical Review* 108: 387–414.

—— (2004), 'Epicurean Equanimity Towards Death.' *Philosophy and Phenomenological Research* 69: 92–114.

EPICURUS. 'Letter to Menoeceus.' Many versions.

FEINBERG, JOEL (1993), 'Harm to Others.' In *The Metaphysics of Death*, ed. John Fischer, 171–90.

FEIT, NEIL (2002), 'The Time of Death's Misfortune.' *Noûs* 36: 359–83.

FELDMAN, FRED (1991), 'Some Puzzles About the Evil of Death.' *The Philosophical Review* 100: 205–27.

—— (1992), *Confrontations with the Reaper: A Philosophical Study of the Nature and Value of Death* (New York: Oxford University Press).

—— (2000a), 'Basic Intrinsic Value.' *Philosophical Studies* 99: 319–45.

—— (2000b), 'The Termination Thesis.' In *Midwest Studies in Philosophy vol. XXIV*, eds. French and Wettstein, 98–115.

—— (2004), *Pleasure and the Good Life: Concerning the Nature, Varieties, and Plausibility of Hedonism* (New York: Oxford University Press).

FISCHER, JOHN (ed.) (1993), *The Metaphysics of Death* (Stanford: Stanford University Press).

—— (1997), 'Death, Badness, and the Impossibility of Experience.' *The Journal of Ethics* 1: 341–53.

—— (2006), 'Epicureanism about Death and Immortality.' *The Journal of Ethics* 10: 355–81.

FRENCH, PETER, AND HOWARD WETTSTEIN (2000), *Midwest Studies in Philosophy vol. XXIV: Life and Death: Metaphysics and Ethics* (Malden, MA: Blackwell Publishers).

GETTIER, EDMUND (1963), 'Is Justified True Belief Knowledge?' *Analysis* 23: 121–3.

GLANNON, WALTER (2001), 'Persons, Lives, and Posthumous Harms.' *Journal of Social Philosophy* 32: 127–42.

GOLDSTEIN, IRWIN (1989), 'Pleasure and Pain: Unconditional, Intrinsic Values.' *Philosophy and Phenomenological Research* 50: 255–76.

GOLDSWORTHY, JEFFREY (1992), 'Well-Being and Value.' *Utilitas* 4: 1–26.

GRANDIN, TEMPLE AND CATHERINE JOHNSON (2005), *Animals in Translation: Using the Mysteries of Autism to Decode Animal Behavior* (New York: Scribner).

GREY, WILLIAM (1999), 'Epicurus and the Harm of Death.' *Australasian Journal of Philosophy* 77: 358–64.

GRIFFIN, JAMES (1986), *Well-Being: Its Meaning, Measurement and Moral Importance* (Oxford: Clarendon Press).

HALL, NED (2007), 'Structural Equations and Causation.' *Philosophical Studies* 132: 109–36.

HARMAN, ELIZABETH (2003), 'The Potentiality Problem.' *Philosophical Studies* 114: 173–98.

—— (2004), 'Can We Harm and Benefit in Creating?' *Philosophical Perspectives* 18: 89–113.

HARMAN, GILBERT (2000), *Explaining Value* (Oxford: Clarendon Press).

HEATHWOOD, CHRIS (2005), 'The Problem of Defective Desires.' *Australasian Journal of Philosophy* 83: 487–504.

—— (Forthcoming), 'Fitting Attitudes and Welfare.' *Oxford Studies in Metaethics*.

—— (Unpublished), 'Subjective Desire Satisfactionism.' Manuscript, University of Colorado.

HERSHENOV, DAVID (2007), 'A More Palatable Epicureanism.' *American Philosophical Quarterly* 44: 170–80.

HETHERINGTON, STEPHEN (2001), 'Deathly Harm.' *American Philosophical Quarterly* 38: 349–62.

HOLTUG, NILS (2001), 'On the Value of Coming Into Existence.' *The Journal of Ethics* 5: 361–84.

HUEMER, MICHAEL (2003), 'Non-Egalitarianism.' *Philosophical Studies* 114: 147–71.

—— (2005), *Ethical Intuitionism* (New York: Palgrave MacMillan).

HUME, DAVID (1740/1978), *A Treatise of Human Nature* (2nd edn., eds. Selby-Bigge and Nidditch) (Oxford: Oxford University Press).

HURKA, THOMAS (1993), *Perfectionism* (New York: Oxford University Press).

—— (1998), 'Two Kinds of Organic Unity.' *The Journal of Ethics* 2: 299–320.

—— (2001), *Virtue, Vice and Value* (New York: Oxford University Press).

JANIS, ALLEN (2006), 'Conventionality of Simultaneity.' *The Stanford Encyclopedia of Philosophy (Fall 2006 Edition)*, Edward N. Zalta (ed.), URL = <http://plato.stanford.edu/archives/fall2006/entries/spacetime-convensimul/>.

JOHANSSON, JENS (2005), *Mortal Beings: On the Metaphysics and Value of Death* (Stockholm: Almqvist & Wiksell International).

KAGAN, SHELLY (1994), 'Me and My Life.' *Proceedings of the Aristotelian Society* 94: 309–24.

—— (1998), 'Rethinking Intrinsic Value.' *The Journal of Ethics* 2: 277–97.

—— (2001), 'Thinking About Cases.' In *Moral Knowledge*, eds. Paul, Miller and Paul (Cambridge: Cambridge University Press), 44–63.

KAGAN, SHELLY and PETER VALLENTYNE (1997), 'Infinite Value and Finitely Additive Value Theory.' *The Journal of Philosophy* 94: 5–26.

KAHN, CHARLES (1985), 'Democritus and the Origins of Moral Psychology.' *The American Journal of Philology* 106: 1–31.

KAMM, FRANCES (1993), *Morality, Mortality, Vol. 1: Death and Whom to Save from It* (New York: Oxford University Press).

KAUFMAN, FREDERIK (2004), 'Pre-Vital and Post-Mortem Nonexistence.' In *Life, Death, & Meaning*, ed. Benatar, 241–64.

KAUFMANN, WALTER (1961), *The Faith of a Heretic* (Garden City, NJ: Doubleday and Co.).

KAWALL, JASON (1999), 'The Experience Machine and Mental State Theories of Well-Being.' *The Journal of Value Inquiry* 33: 381–87.

KELLER, SIMON (2004), 'Welfare and the Achievement of Goals.' *Philosophical Studies* 121: 27–41.

—— (Unpublished), 'Welfare as Success.' Manuscript, Victoria University Wellington.

KIRKHAM, RICHARD (1995), *Theories of Truth* (Cambridge, MA: MIT Press).

KORSGAARD, CHRISTINE (1983), 'Two Distinctions in Goodness.' *The Philosophical Review* 92: 169–95.

—— (1989), 'Personal Identity and the Unity of Agency: A Kantian Response to Parfit.' *Philosophy and Public Affairs* 18: 101–32.

KRAMER, SCOTT AND KUANG-MING WU (eds.) (1988), *Thinking Through Death, Volume I* (Malabar, FL: Robert E. Krieger Publishing Co.).

KRAUT, RICHARD (1994), 'Desire and the Human Good.' *Proceedings and Addresses of the American Philosophical Association* 68: 39–54.

—— (2007), *What is Good and Why: The Ethics of Well-Being* (Cambridge, MA: Harvard University Press).

KRIPKE, SAUL (1972), *Naming and Necessity* (Cambridge, MA: Harvard University Press).

LAMONT, JULIAN (1998), 'A Solution to the Puzzle of When Death Harms Its Victims.' *Australasian Journal of Philosophy* 76: 198–212.

LEMOS, NOAH (2006), 'Indeterminate Value, Basic Value, and Summation.' In *The Good, the Right, Life and Death*, eds. McDaniel *et al.*, 71–82.

LEWIS, C. I. (1948), *An Analysis of Knowledge and Valuation* (LaSalle, IL: Open Court Publishing Co.).

LEWIS, DAVID (1973), *Counterfactuals* (New York: Basil Blackwell).

—— (1979), 'Counterfactual Dependence and Time's Arrow.' *Noûs* 13: 455–76.

—— (1986a), *On the Plurality of Worlds* (New York: Basil Blackwell).

—— (1986b), 'Causation.' In *Philosophical Papers*, vol. II (New York: Oxford University Press), 159–213.

—— (2000), 'Causation as Influence.' *The Journal of Philosophy* 97: 182–97.

LEWIS, DAVID AND RAE LANGTON (1998), 'Defining "Intrinsic."' *Philosophy and Phenomenological Research* 58: 333–45.

LI, JACK (1999), 'Commentary on Lamont's When Death Harms its Victims.' *Australasian Journal of Philosophy* 77: 349–57.

LIPPERT-RASMUSSEN, KASPER (2007), 'Why Killing Some People Is More Seriously Wrong than Killing Others.' *Ethics* 117: 716–38.

LOCKE, JOHN (1689/1975) *An Essay concerning Human Understanding*, ed. Peter H. Nidditch (Oxford: Clarendon Press).

LUCRETIUS (1965), *On Nature*. trans., intro., and notes, Russell Geer (New York: Bobbs-Merrill).

LUPER, STEVEN (2004), 'Posthumous Harm.' *American Philosophical Quarterly* 41: 63–72.

—— (2006), 'Death.' *The Stanford Encyclopedia of Philosophy (Spring 2006 Edition)*, Edward N. Zalta (ed.), URL =<http://plato.stanford.edu/archives/spr2006/entries/death/>.

—— (2007), 'Mortal Harm.' *Philosophical Quarterly* 57: 239–51.

McDANIEL, KRIS, JASON RAIBLEY, RICHARD FELDMAN, AND MICHAEL ZIMMERMAN (eds.) (2006), *The Good, the Right, Life and Death: Essays in Honor of Fred Feldman* (Burlington, VT: Ashgate Publishing).

McDANIEL, KRIS (Unpublished), 'On It Being Better Never to Have Been Born.' Manuscript, Syracuse University.

MACINTYRE, ALASDAIR (1981), *After Virtue* (London: Duckworth).

McMAHAN, JEFF (1988), 'Death and the Value of Life.' *Ethics* 99: 32–61.

—— (2002), *The Ethics of Killing: Problems at the Margins of Life* (New York: Oxford University Press).

MARKOSIAN, NED (2004), 'A Defense of Presentism.' In *Oxford Studies in Metaphysics, vol. 1*, ed. Dean Zimmerman (Oxford: Oxford University Press), 47–82.

MARQUIS, DON (1985), 'Harming the Dead.' *Ethics* 96: 159–61.

—— (1989), 'Why Abortion is Immoral.' *The Journal of Philosophy* 86: 183–202.

MENDOLA, JOSEPH (2006), *Goodness and Justice: A Consequentialist Moral Theory* (New York: Cambridge University Press).

MOORE, G. E. (1903), *Principia Ethica*. Rev. edn (1993) (New York: Cambridge University Press).

—— (1922), *Philosophical Studies* (New York: The Humanities Press, Inc.).

MOTHERSILL, MARY (1999), 'Old Age.' *Proceedings and Addresses of the APA* 73(2): 9–23.

MURPHY, JEFFRIE (1976), 'Rationality and the Fear of Death.' *The Monist* 59: 187–203.

MURPHY, MARK (1999), 'The Simple Desire-Fulfillment Theory.' *Noûs* 33: 247–72.

NAGEL, THOMAS (1979), *Mortal Questions* (New York: Cambridge University Press).

NIETZSCHE, FRIEDRICH (1891), *Thus Spoke Zarathustra*. Many versions.

NORCROSS, ALASTAIR (1997), 'Good and Bad Actions.' *The Philosophical Review* 106: 1–34.

—— (2005), 'Harming in Context.' *Philosophical Studies* 123: 149–73.

NOZICK, ROBERT (1974), *Anarchy, State and Utopia* (New York: Basic Books).

—— (1981), *Philosophical Explanations* (Cambridge, MA: Harvard University Press).

NUSSBAUM, MARTHA (1994), *The Therapy of Desire* (Princeton: Princeton University Press).

OLSON, JONAS (2004a), 'Intrinsicalism and Conditionalism about Final Value.' *Ethical Theory and Moral Practice* 7: 31–52.

—— (2004b), 'Buck-Passing and the Wrong Kind of Reasons.' *Philosophical Quarterly* 54: 295–300.

OVERVOLD, MARK (1980), 'Self-Interest and the Concept of Self-Sacrifice.' *Canadian Journal of Philosophy* 10: 105–18.

PARFIT, DEREK (1984), *Reasons and Persons* (New York: Oxford University Press).

PITCHER, GEORGE (1993), 'The Misfortunes of the Dead.' In *The Metaphysics of Death*, ed. John Fischer, 159–68.

PLATO. *Apology*. Many edns and trans. Cited by standard reference system.

—— *Phaedo*. Many edns and trans. Cited by standard reference system.

PORTMORE, DOUGLAS (2007a), 'Desire Fulfillment and Posthumous Harm.' *American Philosophical Quarterly* 44: 27–38.

—— (2007b), 'Welfare, Achievement, and Self-Sacrifice.' *Journal of Ethics & Social Philosophy* 2: 1–28.

PRIEST, GRAHAM (1998), 'What's So Bad About Contradictions?' *Journal of Philosophy* 95: 410–26.

—— (2004), 'Dialetheism.' *The Stanford Encyclopedia of Philosophy (Summer 2004 Edition)*, Edward N. Zalta (ed.), URL =<http://plato.stanford.edu/archives/sum2004/entries/dialetheism/>.

PRIOR, ARTHUR (1961), 'On a Family of Paradoxes.' *Notre Dame Journal of Formal Logic* 2: 16–32.

RABINOWICZ, WLODEK AND JAN ÖSTERBERG (1996), 'Value Based on Preferences: On Two Interpretations of Preference Utilitarianism.' *Economics and Philosophy* 12: 1–27.

RABINOWICZ, WLODEK AND TONI RØNNOW-RASMUSSEN (1999), 'A Distinction in Value: Intrinsic and For Its Own Sake.' *Proceedings of the Aristotelian Society* 100: 33–51.

RABINOWICZ, WLODEK AND TONI RØNNOW-RASMUSSEN (2004), 'The Strike of the Demon: Fitting Pro-Attitudes and Value.' *Ethics* 114: 391–423.

RAWLS, JOHN (1971), *A Theory of Justice* (Cambridge, MA: Harvard University Press).

ROSENBAUM, STEPHEN (1993), 'How to be Dead and Not Care: A Defense of Epicurus.' In *The Metaphysics of Death*, ed. Fischer, 119–34.

ROSS, W.D. (1930/1988), *The Right and the Good* (Indianapolis, IN: Hackett Publishing Co.).

RUBEN, DAVID-HILLEL (1988), 'A Puzzle about Posthumous Predication.' *The Philosophical Review* 97: 211–36.

RUSSELL, BERTRAND (1908/1971), 'Mathematical Logic as Based on the Theory of Types.' In *Logic and Knowledge* (New York: Capricorn Books).

SCANLON, THOMAS (1998), *What We Owe to Each Other* (Cambridge, MA: Harvard University Press).

SCHAFFER, JONATHAN (2000), 'Trumping Preemption.' *The Journal of Philosophy* 97: 165–81.

—— (2005), 'Contrastive Causation.' *The Philosophical Review* 114: 297–328.

SCHROEDER, TIMOTHY (2004), *Three Faces of Desire* (New York: Oxford University Press).

SIDER, THEODORE (2001), *Four-Dimensionalism: An Ontology of Persistence and Time* (New York: Oxford University Press).

SIDGWICK, HENRY (1907), *The Methods of Ethics*, 7th edn. (Indianapolis, IN: Hackett Publishing Co.).

SILVERSTEIN, HARRY (1980), 'The Evil of Death.' *The Journal of Philosophy* 77: 401–24.

—— (2000), 'The Evil of Death Revisited.' In *Midwest Studies in Philosophy, Volume XXIV*, eds. French and Wettstein, 116–34.

—— (Forthcoming), 'The Time of the Evil of Death.' In *Time and Identity*, eds. Campbell, O'Rourke, and Silverstein.

SINGER, PETER (1999), 'A Response.' In *Singer and his Critics*, ed. Dale Jamieson (Malden, MA: Blackwell Publishers), 269–335.

SINNOTT-ARMSTRONG, WALTER (1997), 'You Can't Lose What You Ain't Never Had: A Reply to Marquis on Abortion.' *Philosophical Studies* 96: 59–72.

SKOW, BRADFORD (2007), 'Are Shapes Intrinsic?' *Philosophical Studies* 133: 111–30.

SOBEL, DAVID AND DAVID COPP (2001), 'Against Direction of Fit Accounts of Belief and Desire.' *Analysis* 61: 44–53.

SORENSEN, ROY (2005), 'The Cheated God: Death and Personal Time.' *Analysis* 65: 119–25.

STALNAKER, ROBERT (1984), *Inquiry* (Cambridge, MA: MIT Press).

STRAWSON, GALEN (2004), 'Against Narrativity.' *Ratio* 17: 428–52.

SUITS, DAVID (2004), 'Why Death Is Not Bad for the One Who Died.' In *Life, Death, & Meaning*, ed. David Benatar, 265–84.

SUMNER, L. W (1996), *Welfare, Happiness, and Ethics* (New York: Oxford University Press).

TÄNNSJÖ, TORBJÖRN (1998), *Hedonistic Utilitarianism* (Edinburgh: Edinburgh University Press).

TAYLOR, JAMES S. (2005), 'The Myth of Posthumous Harm.' *American Philosophical Quarterly* 42: 311–32.

VAYRYNEN, PEKKA (2006), 'Resisting the Buck-Passing Account of Value.' *Oxford Studies in Metaethics* 1: 295–324.

VELLEMAN, DAVID (1993), 'Well-being and Time.' In *The Metaphysics of Death*, ed. John Fischer, 329–57.

WEATHERSON, BRIAN (2007), 'Intrinsic vs. Extrinsic Properties.' *The Stanford Encyclopedia of Philosophy (Spring 2007 Edition)*, Edward N. Zalta (ed.), URL = <http://plato.stanford.edu/archives/spr2007/entries/intrinsic-extrinsic/>.

WILLIAMS, BERNARD (1973), *Problems of the Self* (Cambridge: Cambridge University Press).

—— (1993), 'The Makropulos Case: Reflections on the Tedium of Immortality.' In *The Metaphysics of Death*, ed. John Fischer, 73–92.

WILLIAMS, CHRISTOPHER (2007), 'Death and Deprivation.' *Pacific Philosophical Quarterly* 88: 265–83.

WOODWARD, JAMES (1986), 'The Non-Identity Problem.' *Ethics* 96: 804–31.

YOURGRAU, PALLE (1987), 'The Dead.' *The Journal of Philosophy* 84: 84–101.

INDEX

CPSIA information can be obtained at www.ICGtesting.com
Printed in the USA
BVOW01s0541230816

459876BV00019B/64/P